DISCLAIMER

Use of company and product names is not authorized by, associated with, or sponsored by any trademark owner, and is intended for literary effect only. *The Girl's Guide to Depravity* is a humor book. Its advice and suggestions are not meant to be taken seriously. The author and publisher disclaim all liability in connection with the use of this book.

Books published by Running Press are available at special discounts for bulk purchases in the United States by corporations, institutions, and other organizations. For more information, please contact the Special Markets Department at the Perseus Books Group, 2300 Chestnut Street, Suite 200, Philadelphia, PA 19103, or call (800) 810-4145, ext. 5000, or e-mail special.markets@perseusbooks.com.

ISBN 978-0-7624-4487-8
Library of Congress Control Number: 2011933256

E-book ISBN 978-0-7624-4535-6

9 8 7 6 5 4 3 2 1
Digit on the right indicates the number of this printing

Edited by Jordana Tusman
Designed by Corinda Cook
Typography: Maxima, Kepler, and Bodoni Ornament

Running Press Book Publishers
2300 Chestnut Street
Philadelphia, PA 19103-4371

Visit us on the web!
www.runningpress.com
www.thegirlsguidetodepravity.com

CONTENTS

AUTHOR'S NOTE

The following fuckery was performed by professional sluts and must not be attempted by anyone on the JV team. Be fully aware that recreating some of the actions you're about to read may lead you to be (a) punched in the vagina, (b) banned from the bar, (c) thrown into rehab, (d) arrested, or (e) all of the above. All names, locations, characteristics, and some facts have been changed.

INTRODUCTION

I used to be a good girl. I'm talking no-drinking-before-dark, called-my-mother-every-Sunday, never-took-a-shit-at-a-guy's-house, didn't-fuck-on-the-first-date kind of good girl. I was looking for my soulmate—a guy I imagined would look like a dirty hot Johnny Depp, have an arty job, drive a vintage car, be a bit of a bad boy, and yet still treat me like a princess—and I thought I could find him in the bars and clubs of Hollywood.

I owned every dating book ever published. Most of them advised me to play hard to get, to move on if a guy wasn't calling me first or tripping over himself to ask me out. But no matter how strictly I adhered to these rules, I still got fucked—and not in the good way.

If I played hard to get, he went for someone else. If I waited for him to make the first move, I waited forever. I sat at home alone, checking my cell every five minutes and fighting off the urge to call him incessantly until he picked up, because I was convinced that if he wasn't calling me, he didn't deserve me. But my vagina didn't deserve the severe neglect I was imposing on it by waiting for some guy to swoop in and sweep me off my feet. And I wasn't the only one.

None of my girlfriends who subscribed to this outdated "man pursues woman" philosophy had boyfriends, ever had dates, or were even getting laid. We were a bunch of bored-ass bitches wasting some of our prime fucking years denying our most basic of impulses. Abstaining from having sex with a guy you're creaming for is hard enough, but forcing yourself not to call him constantly, stalk his Facebook page, or bribe a friend of his with whiskey to set you guys up is akin to water torture.

That's when we decided to throw out all our archaic dating books and make our own set of rules, our very own handbook for all us hot, modern-day bitches. That's when *The Girl's Guide to Depravity* was born.

If you're like me (and since you're reading this book, congratulations: either you're on your way or you at least aspire to an awesome level of depravity), you're sick of hearing that it's human nature for the man to take the lead. Sure, men love the chase, but so does a Depraved Girl.* Why should we have to hold back for fear of scaring away the delicate little flower otherwise known as "man"? It's time to take back control, have a little fun, and have a lot of sex—and do it all without getting hurt.

What's the point of wasting your time going on ten dates with a guy before sleeping with him when you can do it on the first date before you have anything invested? Since there's a good chance he's gonna ditch your ass after he gets some anyway, you might as well have it on your own terms—and at least you'll have gotten laid first!

* You can find a definition for this and any word with an asterisk in the Glossary (page 268).

If you're looking for some touchy-feely "respect yourself and your body" bullshit, call your mother. I'm here to tell you to go ahead and do something bad if it feels good, like going on a stalkapalooza* of your latest lust's favorite hangouts or going for the sexy dick over the adorable nice guy.

Because the only thing you have to lose . . . is an orgasm.

IT'S BETTER TO GET FUCKED THAN FUCKED OVER

Most women are looking for love. I say fuck love and just look for sex instead.

Hold up: I fully admit that I need love just as much as the next hooker, but when you go looking for love, you usually end up with a handful of Xannies to dull the pain of his rejection stabbing you like a knife in the heart. However, when you go trawling for some hot monkey sex, you usually find it. Love can be one of the glorious side effects, but if you go searching for nothing more than a good fuck, chances are you won't get fucked over.

I know many a girl who's been strung along by some fickle dick who was all about the romance in the beginning—I'm talking flowers, wine, and condoms ribbed for *her* pleasure—but that's how they trick you. Once they start getting it regularly and you finally think you can relax and cancel your monthly ass-waxing appointment, they switch it up. If he used to text you every day from work, he'll Facebook you late at night. If he used to take you out and spend some cash on you several times a week, he'll tell you to grab yourself some Chipotle before coming over to watch a movie and fuck at his house.

J was my first real love. I met him back in my early days before I was depraved and still believed in things like happily ever after and dental dams. But I was about to get a rude fucking awakening.

He was friends with one of my friend's boyfriends. And after being introduced to him at a party one night, I was sure he was "the one." J had a bit of a bad-boy edge, just what I liked: he was in a band but made his living as a graphic artist, drove a classic BMW, and was friends with all the bartenders.

I followed all the good-girl rules: I never called him first, pretended to have other plans when he asked me out, and absolutely was not going to have sex with him until after we'd been on at least three dates.

But I felt myself falling for him after only the first date. It wasn't hard because he adored me. I'm talking called me every day, made up songs about me, bought me quirky gifts "just because" adored me.

And even though when we'd make out my vag* would get wetter than the Pacific, I still clung to my three-date rule. He said he respected me for that. And when we finally did do the do? Oh. My. God. The most amazing sex I'd ever had, not just physically, but emotionally.

He told me I was the kind of girl he could see himself marrying one day. And one night after we'd been together only a month, he told me he loved me. Of course, it was in a drunken stupor after I had just sucked the life out of him, but still.

He even introduced me to his family. When his sister came from Seattle for a visit, she and I became besties over two bottles of wine the day he got stuck at work. Although I had been trained to try not to think about (and definitely never talk about) the future with a man for fear of scaring him off, he began to bring it up. He talked about taking a trip to Spain together in the summer, adopting a dog together, and maybe even moving in together.

Then he disappeared. He stopped calling me, stopped texting me, and stopped e-mailing me altogether. I wondered if he had died or gotten horribly hurt in some accident and was in a hospital somewhere trying to call me but couldn't use his arms. But my friend said her boyfriend had just seen him and he was fine.

What had I done wrong? I analyzed our last few conversations over and over again wondering if I had pissed him off in some way. I cried to my friends over Ben & Jerry's, trying not to call him and ask him what happened. "He's just not into you anymore," they told me, telling me I deserved better and to forget about him and move on. Easier said than done.

They soon grew sick of my pity party* of one and stopped returning my sobbing calls in the middle of the night. Even my mom told me to nut up and stop bawling like a baby. No one wanted to be around me anymore.

Unable to sleep, eat, or even watch the trashy TV shows I used to love, I soon found myself spending my nights drinking alone at my neighborhood bar. That's where I met S. She was older, wiser, and as I would soon find out, completely depraved. I told her my sob story one night over drinks she had scored from some douche before she made him get lost.

I fully expected her to tell me to forget about him and move on because he was clearly no longer interested, but to my surprise, she said just the opposite. She told me I should call him every fifteen minutes until he told me why he dumped me. And if he didn't return any of my calls, I should stalk him until I found out. I deserved to know, she told me.

It was the first piece of advice I had been given that actually made me feel better. It gave me a purpose, something to do with my time other than sit around wondering what the fuck had happened. Now I was finally going to *know* what happened.

I launched my phone assault that night. Obvs, I got no response. When I reported back to her at the bar the next night, she said we should waste no time moving into phase two: stalking. We got the bartender to make us some super-sized vodka Red Bulls in a to-go cup and parked ourselves outside of his empty apartment.

After several hours and two piss squats, he still wasn't home. Our vodka Red Bulls had long been drunk and I was having a hard time keeping my eyes open. That's when S gave me my first Ritalin. Have you ever been with someone the first time they were on speed? Yeah, I was that annoying, but to S's credit, she just let me talk and work my jaw like a meth head on a three-day binge.

He finally turned into his driveway at four a.m.—with a girl in his front seat. My heart sank, but S kept me on task, which was very easy to do in my speedy state. It was too dark to see who she was, so S suggested we go inside for a sneak attack. She asked me if he had given me a key to the place, but of course he hadn't. Then I remembered the one time we were together when he had locked himself out and had to break into his apartment through a window.

When we stumbled in, we could hear the unmistakable sounds of sucking and fucking coming from his bedroom. I was frozen, but S pushed me forward, urging me to confront the bastard. I threw open the door and was shocked to see who he was in bed with.

"You're having sex with your sister???" I exclaimed, about to puke in my mouth. "Sister, my dick," said S under her breath.

After their initial surprise wore off and S threatened to take a dump on top of his precious BMW if he didn't tell me the truth, I finally found out what had been going on. Obviously, this bitch was not his sister. He had been cheating on me with her the whole time we were together. When she had come out to visit, she had decided to move down here. The day she arrived was the last time I ever heard from him.

Now, I had heard horrendous stories of deception like this before, but I couldn't believe that it would happen to me, and that someone I loved and thought loved me back could be that much of a dick.

As we left him and his "sister" to continue having incestuous sex, S scooped up some dog shit from a nearby lawn and piled it up on top of his car. "Fuck him," she shrugged.

The next night I was back at my neighborhood bar with S, still a little shell-shocked over what we had found. But I had gotten my closure and no longer craved to talk with him—or any man for that matter. I needed a time-out to get over my heartbreak.

"You got fucked over. But that shouldn't stop you from getting fucked," S said. She was right.

I hung out with S for the rest of the summer, which became my summer of Xantinis* and one-night-stands. I'm not going to

try to pretend I never got fucked over again or didn't fall for some dick when I should have known better. But at least I had the time of my life filling up on sex, prescription drugs, and free drinks in the meantime.

As for S, the last time I saw her was at the end of the summer when she ended up in the hospital getting her stomach pumped after taking one too many sleeping pills to counteract all the Ritalin and Red Bulls. Her parents threw her in rehab in Arizona where she "found God." I hear she's still stalking people—but now it's in the name of Jesus.

BE THE LAST WOMAN STANDING

If you wanna get the guy, you better be prepared to stay at the bar, the club, the party, even work until the bitter end. Because good dick is hard to find, and if you're not willing to put in the time, there'll be another bitch who will.

Sure, when you see him ramming his tongue down the throat of a Megan Fox look-alike at the party, it's tempting to pack it in, go home, and eat the rest of those pot brownies you were saving for a rainy day, but don't. A well-placed herpes rumor by a great friend just might take her out of the running, and then you'll be sad you didn't stay to become his sloppy seconds.

Once I was on a weekend stalkapalooza of my loser crush of the moment. After two straight days of drinking and hangovers, I finally found him Monday night at Bigfoot Lodge.

When I spotted him, he was chatting up this bitchy anorexic girl, who, incidentally, had slept with two of my friends' boyfriends. She was looking at him like he was the one M&M she had for lunch, but I wasn't deterred.

I stuck by his side as he ordered round after round, but the rex* wasn't budging either. She matched me vodka tonic for vodka tonic. Now anyone who's ever had a drink with me knows I can't hold my liquor, but I was damned if I was gonna lose a drinking competition to a ninety-pound whore!

As he got up to get us more drinks I turned to her and said, "Look bitch, I outweigh you by twenty-five pounds and I have a pair of Depends in my purse so I can sit here *allll* night."

"Well, I was social chair for my sorority at ASU, so that means I have a degree in getting fucked up," she responded, a surprisingly steely look in her eye for someone so devoid of substance.

We went a few more rounds, and by last call, she was swaying and staggering. When she finally got up to empty her pea-sized bladder, I followed her to the bathroom, where I bribed an alkie* to hold the door shut and not let her out under any circumstances.

Then I went out and told my crush she had left with someone else. I was the last woman standing, so he ended up taking me home. Sure, I puked in his bed and he kicked me out before the P went into the V, but at least I won!

Ladies: don't go into battle uninformed. If you can't tell just by looking at her, here's how you can identify what kind of skank you're dealing with by what she's drinking:

ID YOUR COMPETITION BY THEIR COCKTAILS

Sluts	Lite beer, mojitos, anything in a shot glass
Bitches	Martini, red wine, vodka soda
Douchebaguettes	Long Island iced tea, margaritas, Goldschläger
College Girls	Sex on the beach, Jell-O shots, kamikaze, buttery nipple, anything frozen
Gold Diggers	The most expensive drink at the bar
Good Girls	Half a glass of white wine, water
Pumas	Cosmopolitan, apple martini, anything that was popular fifteen years ago
Depraved Girl	Whiskey, vodka tonics, any top-shelf alcohol she didn't have to pay for, something she can easily slip a roofie or Viagra into if she needs to dose her target

FREE DRINKS ALWAYS TASTE BETTER

I know you're all Miss Independent women, women who can buy themselves their own drinks thank-you-very-much, women who will blow half their paycheck on a Missoni scarf or laser hair removal to obtain a perfect, lifelong Hitler 'stache over their gash, but let's be honest: free drinks just taste better.

Sometimes, a girl just wants to have a quiet drink with a friend alone, and doesn't want to be bothered by some loser trying to buy her time—but girls, a free drink from a loser is still a free drink. Plus, how can you get into trouble if you're drinking alone?

The next time you're about to order yourself a drink at the bar, instead:

- Make eye contact with someone at the bar. Sometimes a little eye contact is all the encouragement a guy needs.
- Wait until he orders, then sidle right up next to him and say, "I've been trying to get the bartender's attention all night!" Make sure you do it before the drinks are delivered so he can tack your order onto his.
- Sometimes a simple "buy me a drink" does the trick. Extra points if you get him to buy you top-shelf liquor.

After one of my girlfriend K's particularly painful breakups, we decided to take our usual pity party to our local bar. The minute we walked in the door, a dude who looked as if he had been headed for the nearest Margaritaville, but took a wrong turn somewhere, offered to buy us a drink.

Of course we immediately asked for a split of Veuve. He turned to the bartender and ordered us two vodka tonics. "What the fuck?" said my friend. "We don't even rate call drinks?" Of course, we gulped down our well drinks anyway. But then two young douchebaguettes with fake tans, fake tits, fake hair, and fake teeth walked in. We watched in astonishment as Mr. Margaritaville ordered them two Patron Cadillac margaritas.

If my girl wasn't already feeling shiteous from being dumped, the indignity of being offered a well drink while some bargain-basement hos got top-shelf tequila was almost too much for her to bear. So she became determined to get some poor asshole to buy us a split of Veuve by the end of the night.

I can't tell you how many disgusting dudes we talked to that night. I still shudder every time I think of how Psoriasis Man shed some skin flakes into the white wine spritzer he tried to pass off as a glass of bub. But the vomit taste in my mouth was nothing compared to how I felt for my friend, who was bad off enough after getting dumped by her dirty hot boyfriend, not to mention being denied top-shelf booze by far lesser men.

But we wouldn't go thirsty for long. She went to the bathroom and by the time she returned, a split of Veuve was waiting for her at the bar. "Well done, whore!" she said, reaching for a glass. "Oh, this was all you," I responded, explaining that the hot guy with the ironic mustache at the end of the bar had sent it over for her. She headed over to thank him. And by "thank him," I mean took him home and fucked him. I never had the heart to tell her that I was the one who actually bought her the Champagne.

HOW TO DITCH A CLINGER

Okay, so you've scored your drink, and now you've been cornered by a stage-five clinger. A dirty hot guy who is so your type just walked into the bar. How do you lose the loser so you can pounce on six feet of man meat?

Just use one of my fave depraved excuses:

"Do you see anything weird on my lip? No? Oh, good, I forgot to take my Valtrex today and I thought I was getting an outbreak."

"They say you shouldn't drink when you're pregnant, but I think that's total bullshit, don't you?" (This one must be performed with drink in hand.)

"What are you doing tomorrow morning? I want to introduce you to my parents!"

And my personal favorite:

"I would totally fuck you but I just had an abortion this morning and I'm still bleeding like crazy!"

DEPRAVED GIRLS NEVER APOLOGIZE

All's fair in sex and revenge. That's why a Depraved Girl will never apologize for anything done in the heat of battle. I'm not saying we're never wrong, but an apology is an admission of defeat. And Depraved Girls don't go down without a fight—unless free drinks are involved.

I once found myself in a situation that might have made a lesser Depraved Girl beg forgiveness. I was at one of my homes away from home (i.e., my neighborhood dive bar) when I over-heard a guy complaining about how he and his girlfriend hadn't had sex in six months. Six months??? I almost did a spit take of my martini, but it was Armadale vodka and I didn't want to waste a single drop.

I turned around and asked him if that was six months without any sex or if she at least gave him a BJ every night. He said no. HJ?* Nope. FJ?* Nada. RJ?* (Think about that one.) He said he got absolutely no lovin' from her at all in half a year and he wasn't getting much inspiration from his porn collection. I said I knew how to inspire him, then leaned over and whispered into his ear the details of this sex move I do that I like to call the Candyland. Now I won't divulge my secrets (that's for another handbook), but let's just say he practically jizzed in his pants right then and there.

I took him home and after the first five-minute round (don't judge; he hadn't had sex in six months!!!), we fucked all night.

The next day, he broke up with his girlfriend. To celebrate, he and I decided to have the nastiest, kinkiest sex ever. I'm talking ball-gag shit. He fucking loved it. I even snapped a few pics when he was passed out because I didn't think any of my girlfriends would believe a guy had let me do that to him—all in one night. After that, we barely left my house for weeks except to go to work and to get more condoms.

Soon his ex-girlfriend's friends started shitting all over my Facebook wall. They began leaving comments like "low-life skank!" and "no-class boyfriend-stealer!" Instead of deleting them, I simply responded, "Don't hate on me because your girl doesn't know how to please her man!" But then I got a comment back: "She's been going through chemo for the last six months, you bitch!"

I stole the boyfriend of Cancer Girl? This guy had definitely fucked her over at a time when she was too sick to fuck.

I wasn't going to apologize to her because I really hadn't done anything wrong. But he had. I took out an ad in the back of the *LA Weekly* advertising cheap massages using one of the kinkiest pics of him I had taken from our ball-gag night. I made sure they had his correct number, then immediately programmed my phone to block all his future calls.

When the ad was published, I clipped it out and sent it to Cancer Girl at the chemo ward with a two-word note: "You're welcome."

DEPRAVED GIRL NON-APOLOGY APOLOGIES

I'M SORRY you have a complex about your small dick.

I'M SORRY I used the spare key you left at my house after we broke up to move your car to a tow-away zone. You can pick it up at the impound tomorrow.

I'M SORRY you bought all your clothes in 1999.

I'M SORRY I left my flatiron plugged in next to the Juicy T-shirt of that skank you were cheating on me with and the entire apartment caught on fire.

I'M SORRY I switched your shampoo with Nair and you look like that now.

THERE IS NO FRIEND IN EX-BOYFRIEND

I never understood girls who continued to be friends with their exes long after the fucking stopped.

Maybe it's because I've mostly dated assholes, but why on earth would I want to get coffee or go shopping or see a movie with a man whose primary function in my life was to make me scream with pleasure, and then scream with disgust when I found out he was sleeping with that skanky stripper behind my back?

Besides, when I saw him again at the bar after another drunken night of depravity, I'd get to take him home and have hot hate-sex instead of just a friendly fuck. Bonus!

But my sweet friend D didn't really see it that way. She always remained friends with her exes, she told me, as a kind of insurance. Her friendship was a premium that she thought might someday pay off in the renewal of their relationship.

Her most recent breakup was one of those soft breakups. You know the kind when you're too lame to just come out and tell someone you don't want to fuck them anymore so you tell them you "need some time"? That's never been my style—I'm usually about as hard as a porn cock—but that's exactly what happened to D when her boyfriend told her he needed to find himself and he didn't want to be in a relationship at the moment. Being the sweetheart that she is, D told him she completely understood and hoped that they could still be friends. D was an amazing friend. She's the kind of girl who buys you little gifts "just because" and offers to feed your pet ferret when you go on vacation.

Well, her ex was only too eager to take her up on her ferret-feeding offer when he planned a trip to Costa Rica to "find himself."

On the first day of his vacay, D let herself into his apartment with the key that he had given her, armed with $100 worth of brand-spanking-new ferret toys. She fed his little weasel and then looked around his disgustingly dirty apartment and decided to clean up. His ferret stuck by her side as she did all his dishes in the kitchen, vacuumed his carpet in the living room, and then finally went into the bedroom.

She was about to make his disheveled bed when she noticed dirty cheese-filled panties stuffed between the pillows and a condom wrapper on the floor. Apparently, her ex had gone to find himself between the legs of another girl. And a girl who wore cotton bikini briefs with the word *PINK* across the butt. The sweetest girl I knew suddenly became enraged.

DEPRA∨ED fact

Sixty-three percent of girls who remain friends with their ex-boyfriends become crazy cat ladies.

"He knew I would be coming over and he couldn't bother to pick that shit up!?" she said to me later. "It's like he was flaunting his fuck fest in front of my face!"

She felt something in her snap, she said. She opened his window, grabbed the panties, and threw them out the window. She did the same to the condom wrapper. Then she grabbed all the sheets and blankets, wadded them up, and threw them out the window as well, before she could stop herself. She said as soon as she let the tangle of sheets go she realized: his ferret had been sitting on his bed. She was too afraid to look out the tenth-story window to see if there was a crime scene beneath her.

She simply closed the window, gathered up all her toys, and hoofed it out of there. And she never befriended an ex again.

WHERE THERE'S A PILL, THERE'S A WAY

I'm all for enhanced fucking. That's why I won't hesitate to medicate when the circumstances call for it. But, there are some situations that even the most Depraved Girl can't control through manipulation, alcohol, and a strict adherence to these rules. So what's the harm in having a little help?

I once found myself in need of such medicinal assistance when I was coming down off a three-day Vegas bender that involved a swingers' club and a dirty stripper who worked at a club way off the strip called Little Darlings.

It was a Sunday night and I could barely lift my fingers onto my keyboard to untag all the incriminating photos my friends had posted on Facebook when I saw it: my latest stalkee had just checked into the Burgundy Room on Cahuenga.

I was exhausted, but I knew I might not have another opportunity. So I popped a Ritalin, gave myself a whore's bath,* and put on my fuck-me pumps to head out to the bar.

When I got there, he was miraculously alone, yet drunk enough to welcome my company. In fact, he even offered to buy me one of what he was having: a white Russian. I can't refuse a free drink (or his attention), so I happily downed it—even though I'm lactose intolerant. After three or four more rounds of the dude's favorite drink, I felt my stomach gurgling a bit, but he was good to go home and fuck, so I poured an entire bottle of Imodium down my throat and we headed to his house.

Of course, when we got there, he was so wasted that he could barely get it up. This could have been a real problem if he hadn't had an emergency stash of Viagra. He took a little blue pill, and soon enough, his dick was standing at attention.

We had that kind of giggly, drunken sex that seems to go on for hours. Okay, it actually did go on for hours because that's how long his dick stayed hard. I knew I'd have a helluva bangover* the next day, but I was determined to ride him until he exploded, which he eventually did in such a fantastic fashion that the condom ripped.

So as soon as the pharmacy opened, I got my ass in line and washed down the morning-after pill with my morning latte.

I spent the rest of the day at work tending to my four-day hangover, my bangover, and the serious period cramps the morning-after pill was bringing on (by taking a fistful of Motrin, of course), all while constantly checking my phone to see if he had texted me yet.

By the end of the work day, he still hadn't texted me, and the pit* was in full effect. I could have spent the rest of the night being anxious and wondering why he wasn't calling me, or I could have taken a Xanax and gone right to sleep. Which one do you think I did?

Forget diamonds; dolls are a Depraved Girl's best friend. So pay a visit to your pharmacist (a.k.a. your dealer) and make sure you're well stocked for stalking!

HOW TO CURE A BANGOVER

Let's face it, girls: we're not always as flexible as we'd like to be. After pulling an all-night hot-and-heavy humping session, sometimes we wake up in the morning to find ourselves with the worst bangover of our lives. So how do you make it to the morning meeting when you can barely walk straight?

• Neosporin is your friend. Use it generously on the inner and outer lips. Yes, using the slippery substance can also make you hot and horny, but resist the urge to jack it; your vag needs a break.

• That vibe* you carry in your slag-bag*? It makes a great jaw massager when you can barely close your mouth after some serious sucking and fucking.

• DO NOT WEAR A THONG! If you just had some vigorous butt sex, you'll regret it. Trust.

• If all else fails, a little "hair of the dog" never hurt. Call in sick and climb back on that horse!

RX FOR DEPRAVITY

Drug	Prescribed Usage	Depraved Usage
Ritalin	A psycho-stimulant used for the treatment of attention-deficit hyperactivity disorder.	Helps you to stay up all night when you're on a stalkapalooza of your latest lust. Also helpful in curing hangovers, allowing you to drink again.
Valtrex	An anti-viral drug that helps control the symptoms of herpes.	A great tool to humiliate your rivals and frenemies.
Viagra	A drug used to treat erectile dysfunction.	A drug used to help drunken guys get it up. Also can be crushed and dissolved into a drink when a man isn't quite as interested in having sex with you as you'd like.

RX FOR DEPRAVITY

Drug	Prescribed Usage	Depraved Usage
Vicodin	Pain reliever.	Popular recreational drug (especially when paired with alcohol) that's a great bartering tool.
Xanax	A sedative that treats anxiety disorder and panic attacks.	Eliminates "the pit." Also a great garnish to a martini, making it a Xantini.
Rohypnol	A powerful sedative used to treat severe insomnia.	A common date rape drug, Rohypnol, or roofies, can be slipped into someone's drink, turning whatever they're drinking into a roofie colada.*

THE BEST WAY TO GET OVER A GUY IS TO GET UNDER ANOTHER GUY

I'm sure most people will tell you that time is the only thing that helps heal a broken heart, right? Fuck that.

You can go country on his car; you can gain five pounds (all from wine) sitting around watching the entire box set of *Sex and the City*; you can pop Xannies like they're candy; you can eat nothing but Pinkberry for a whole month—but nothing helps you get over a guy as much as getting underneath another guy does.

After one particularly heinous breakup, I tried all of the above—in one night. I ended up spending the wee hours of the morning puking up a pinkish mix of red wine, plain fro-yo, and Xanax chunks while trying to keep my roommate's cat from licking up my puke.

To make things even worse, all I could think about were the dozen strawberry cupcakes with sprinkles he had bought me for my last birthday (it was the only damn thing he ever gave me), trapping me in this loop of puking, sobbing, and pussy-swatting on my bathroom floor.

The next night, I was all set to unhinge, binge, purge, and re-peat when my good friend M came over and forced me into a pair of skinny jeans. Luckily, I had been on the breakup diet for about a week, so they actually fit without my flesh cupcake-ing over the side, and she dragged my sorry ass to the Village Idiot.

That's when I met the Irish musician. He was tall, sexy, and best of all, he had an accent that reminded me of my favorite Colin

Farrell movie—his sex tape. Despite the fact that I SO was not in the mood for another man's dick, M suggested that we all go back to my place for another drink after the bar closed, and then drove off the minute me and Lucky Charms got out of the car.

I guess the one good thing about hooking up with Euros is that they don't care if you're waxed/shaved/vajazzled*/coherent. I had had just the right combination of Xanax and vodka tonics at this point, so after a little bit of wrestling on my couch, we got down to doing the dirty. I can't say it was the best sex I've ever had in my life (he had this annoying habit of talking dirty in ebonics), but it did the trick.

The next day, I was no longer obsessing about the ex. Since the leprechaun hadn't returned my text in, like, five hours, I started obsessing about him instead. I believe in psychology this is called transference.

DEPRAVED fact

Ninety percent of men in bars feel that women should get underneath them to get over their last boyfriend. The remaining 10 percent would rather fuck your ex-boyfriend.

Sure, after another few months of my ~~stalking~~ dating him, he pretty much pulled down his pants and took a dump right on top of my heart, but this time, instead of reaching for the baseball bat and a handful of pills, I pulled on my skinny jeans and headed out to the local meat market to find another peen* to help me mend my broken heart.

NEVER MAKE A GUY FRIEND IF THERE'S NO BENEFITS

Whoever said men are only friends with women they want to sleep with is right. Yet I see bitches left and right making pals with guys they'd never in a million years sleep with.

So ladies, before you accept that friend request from the unfuckable poor guy who shared his outlet with you at Starbucks, ask yourself if a friendship would be beneficial to you in any way. And I'm not just talking about sexually, although that would be my primary reason to make a guy friend.

There are several types of guys who may become friends with benefits:

The Backup Guy: If you were fucking him, he'd be your fuck buddy, but instead you slap the "friends" label on this dude in the event that your fuck buddy sprains his dick or decides to start fucking someone else instead of you. Your backup guy is almost as hot as your fuck buddy, but will become just as hot once you're desperate enough (and have enough vodka sodas). But until then, you can enjoy him buying you free drinks and sending you a few dirty texts.

The Rich Guy: You wouldn't even fuck him with *my* vagina, but this type of guy is always springing for bottle service (the gold medal of free drinks) or offering to pay for you and your girlfriends to join him in Vegas. You probably need to lead him on with the promise of one day getting a crack at your snatch in order to get him to pay your rent or credit card bills, but the Botox you can buy with your extra dough is so worth it.

The Door Guy/Bartender/Barista, etc.: He might not be bone-worthy OR rich, but what he's lacking in hotness and cash money, he makes up for in trade. It pays to be friends with the door guy when you sail right to the front of the line while the twenty skanks who are waiting to get into the hot new club are turning green—and not just from the mix of Prozac, Red Bull, Ritalin, and cocaine they had for dinner. Don't want to wait in the twenty-minute coffee line with all the annoying hipsters at Intelligentsia? Your FWB* has your nonfat double cap ready for you the minute you walk in the door. And anyone, guy OR girl, who supplies you with alcohol is an immediate friend for life.

GUY FRIEND PROS AND CONS

Guy Friend	Pro	Con
The Backup Guy	He's always available when you need a good fuck.	His pathetic dog-eyed looks get tiresome.
The Rich Guy	All-expenses-paid vacay to St. Bart's.	Sooner or later he's going to date-rape you.
The Door Guy	Those jealous looks you get from all the sluts standing in line that you just breeze past on your way into the club.	Who wants to hang out with a three-hundred-pound gorilla?
Bartender	Free drinks!!	You might have to pretend to be interested in his model/acting/whatever aspirations.
Barista	Free drinks!!	"You have a friend who works at Starbucks?"

VIBRATORS MAKE THE BEST BOYFRIENDS

Don't get me wrong: NOTHING can replace a hot dick when you need a good fuck, but unlike the man attached to that glorious appendage, a vibrator will never let you down. While most of my relationships with men lasted a mere matter of months, I've had several long-term relationships with a variety of vibes.

The Plug-in: Big, sturdy, and incredibly reliable, this vibe is the loyal boyfriend you'll probably never have. It's not particularly compact or portable and can often disguise itself as a back massager, but it packs the biggest punch. Kind of like the big stocky guy who breaks you down with his incredible personality, not to mention his amazing tongue dexterity. You may be more attracted to sleeker, battery-powered vibes, but you'll always come back to your trusty plug-in. It doesn't travel well, so you'll never have to worry about losing it. It's something big and strong to snuggle up to under the covers on a cold night or while you're watching a (porno) movie.

The Rabbit: The flashiest vibe, the rabbit will pull you in with its smooth surface and promise of a double orgasm (clit and penetration) action. But just like a hot guy who looks great but isn't as amazing in bed, the rabbit doesn't quite live up to its promise. And you practically need a pilot's license to figure out the controls, which reminds me of this pretty-boy I once hooked up with after a night of getting wasted on sake bombs at the sushi house. I was pretty pleased with myself for being able to pull such a hottie that I didn't mind that he wanted me to tug on his balls while sucking him off AND sticking a finger up his ass. This vibe looks so good that it's great for making other bitches jealous. In fact, I once caught my roommate trying to steal my hunny bunny, but just like I might try to convince a girl who's hot for my man that he's gay, I got her to step off by telling her my vibe had seen plenty of ass.

The Pocket Rocket: Small and discreet, this vibrator is like the short guy you're ashamed you're fucking. You can conceal this little lover just about anywhere: your purse, pocket, or desk drawer when you need that afternoon pick-me-up, and no one will be the wiser. I once steady-fucked a guy like that. He would meet me anywhere, anytime I wanted to get off. He was nice enough, but not particularly hot, and I saw no reason to take him out anywhere my other potential fucks would spot us. As is usually the case when you're not interested, he was desperate to turn our strictly-sex relationship into something more serious, but I constantly put him off with excuses like "it's a really bad time for me because my house just burned down and I need to get my dog a face-lift and I just stopped taking the pill so I'm on a ninety-day period." He eventually grew tired of my shit and broke things off. Now he's married to a gorge* former-model-turned-philanthropist. Go figure. I guess one woman's pocket rocket is another woman's plug-in.

HOW TO MACGYVER A VIBRATOR OUT OF HOUSEHOLD ITEMS

A vibrator can be a girl's best friend. But what happens when you're really horny and your trusty vibe runs out of batteries? Or you loaned it out to your neighbor for her Caribbean vacay, and she won't be back for another three days?

Well, don't worry, girls, several common household items found around the kitchen, bath, and laundry room can be MacGyvered into a vibrator when you just have to get off.

- **Cell Phone:** Duh. Set it to vibrate and make sure you've got a home phone or a good friend who will dial over and over and over until you answer the call.
- **Hand Mixer:** It already resembles the Hitachi Magic Wand (the Cadillac of vibes), so plug in and go! Just make sure you use the top end; you wouldn't want to give yourself a clitoridectomy with those blades.
- **Washing Machine:** Wait until it hits spin cycle, then go rub your vag up against it like it's Johnny Depp! It may take a whole roll of quarters to get you off, but slow and steady wins the orgasm race.
- **Electric Toothbrush:** I've tried this one before and it works. Of course, you probably know better than to use the bristled end . . . my mouth tasted like vagina for about a week after.
- **The Schick Quattro TrimStyle:** A razor and waterproof bikini trimmer in one. Like the geniuses at Schick didn't know what would happen when women stepped into the shower with one of these vibrating babies! Again, watch the blades.

NEVER UNDERESTIMATE THE POWER OF ASKING FOR WHAT YOU WANT

I love the hunt as much as the next Depraved Girl. I've been known to wait hours in the Barney's Warehouse sale line to buy something I don't need that doesn't fit just to get the deal.

But while the chase can really get your heart pumping, which can also lead to some pumping of another kind, sometimes you just don't have the time or energy to chase down your next fuck. We busy bitches have other shit to do—like plotting revenge against a cheating ex, or getting our assholes bleached.

So when you're starving, but too tired to chase down your prey, pull up to the drive-thru window instead and place your order.

Some of you may be reluctant to step up to a dude you've never met and offer NSA* sex, worried they'd be put off by such an aggressive girl. But you're not trying to get a marriage proposal (if you are, you may be reading the wrong book). This is the fast food of fucking we're talking about here.

And the best thing about this technique is that it works just as well with guys who you'd normally think would be out of your league.

One night after a hellish day at work, followed by the news that my best Depraved Girl was hanging up her vagina and getting married, I stopped at the nearest bar and ordered a drink. I considered working my game on either of the guys sitting next to me, but it had been that kind of day and I just couldn't be bothered. But still, I needed to get off.

The annoying sound of a dumb blonde girl laughing (yes, sometimes you can "hear" hair color) pulled my attention to the middle of the bar. Suddenly a light shone on THE hottest piece of male ass you have ever seen, holding court with about three or four gorge yet slightly anorexic chicks. He looked like a male model, not like the skinny waif-boy male models, but the kind that appear on the cover of fitness magazines.

Now, I was wearing my businesswomen's special outfit of pencil skirt, pumps, and a silk tank. Hardly dressed-to-get-laid, but I didn't care. I walked straight up to the group, pushed one of the rexes aside, and whispered into his ear: "Wanna fuck?" It took him approximately 3.4 seconds to decide to ditch the skanks and walk out of the bar with me.

Which is, incidentally, the same amount of time he spent going down on me, but since he had given up drinking to keep his carbs down, his peen worked, and that's all that mattered.

No, I never saw him again—in person—but he appeared in so many ad campaigns and editorials in the months after that he gave me additional spank material for years.

DEPRAVED fact

The odds of getting what you want from a man by asking are 1:1. The odds of getting what you want from a man by hoping he figures it out are 1:1,000.

IT ISN'T
COCK-BLOCKING
IF HE'S
NOT TRYING
TO SCORE

Sorry, girls: you may have seen him first, but I'm not cock-blocking you if his peen has no interest in connecting with your vag.

My friends and I pretty much subscribe to the five-second rule when it comes to guys. You have exactly five seconds to get him to cream for you; otherwise, he's fair game. I never understood those girls who would call dibs on a totally fuckable dude the very first second they saw him, and even if he found her as repulsive as a dirty tampon, none of her friends could get on him. EVER.

The difference between a girl like that and a Depraved Girl is that the DG would never stand in the way of her girlfriend getting to bust a nut with some random hottie just because she couldn't close the deal. Because at least the delicious details she'll get from her girlfriend afterward will give her a 'gasm* by proxy. That's why it's okay to put dicks before chicks.

I was once involved in a hottie tug-of-war with a competing crew of bitches. My girls and I were enjoying our usual Thursday night special of Xantinis and man-grabbing when N spotted this gorge guy sitting by himself at the end of the bar. She busted out her standard move—the ass-grab—but the guy must have been uber-grumpy because he was not having any of her smooth lines or roving hands.

But he was just too delicious to waste, so N retreated and was about to tag me in when he was swarmed by three uptight-looking cunts. You know, the kind that look like thirty-year-old sorority sisters? They were all looking at him like he was the last pair of size seven Manolos at a sample sale, but they let the blondest one take the lead.

Amused, I lingered nearby as she tried desperately to engage in some witty banter, but he couldn't take his eyes off her little friend. We watched as it became obvious to her that he wasn't going to bite, and waited for her to give the go-ahead to her friend, but instead of the slight nod we were looking for, she pretty much gave the girl a look that said, "I'll open up your Louis Vuitton bag and take a shit inside it if you even think about it," so the girls just turned and headed to their own corner of the bar.

That's when I made my move, but not without a little encouragement from N, who told me to take off my heels and make sure I kept my hands to myself. I heeded her advice and came at him with a fake story about how annoyed I was after some guy had tried to cop a feel. We commiserated over shots of Patron. And then we went home and commiserated over a three-hour sex marathon.

The next morning, hungover and bangedover, I met N for a bloody Mary at our favorite brunch place where I gave her every single dirty detail of the dirty deed.

HOOKUP STRATEGY		
Guy's Approach	**Girl's Approach**	**Depraved Girl's Approach**
Get hottest girl to sleep with you.	If you don't get laid, no one does.	Get anyone on your crew laid.

ALWAYS BE PREPARED

You never know where your next fuck is coming from. That's why you've always gotta be prepared for a night of super-sex, whether you're just going to the grocery store or visiting Grandpa in the old folks' home (don't judge).

Prepare your face: If you are one of the very few lucky sluts who roll out of bed looking fit to be tied up, then fuck you. But if you're like the rest of us, you need at least some blush, eyeliner, and mascara in order to hide the damage of the liquid dinner you had last night.

Prepare your vag: Unless you like to rock the full-on seventies bush, make sure you're always freshly waxed. If you have the time and money, laser hair removal makes this a no-brainer (and a no-puber). If shaving's your thing, you might want to do it every day. No guy wants beard burn from your clam beard.

Prepare your slag-bag: Also known as a ho-kit,* this should be a compact little bag you keep with you in your purse or car that's full of one-night-stand supplies. Condoms, toothbrush, gum, Anal Eaze—whatever you may need to make your slutventures* comfortable.

I once broke this cardinal rule of depravity at my cousin's bar mitzvah. Knowing I'd be surrounded by hundreds of prepubescent boys, I decided that I didn't need to wash the stink of the previous night of debauchery out of my snatch and didn't even bother bringing my slag-bag (the supplies of which needed replenishing anyway; it was a particularly slutty time in my life). I had always had a thing for one of my older cousins—no blood relation; I'm not *that* depraved—who was looking hotter than ever.

By the time the band started to play the horah, I was playing the whore-ah with my hot cuz in the back of his Benz. He kept trying to pull my dress over my head, but knowing I had a bad case of BO and had left my deodorant in my ho-kit at home, I convinced him that my zipper was stuck.

We both fumbled around for a condom that neither one of us had. So we agreed on oral, and after flipping a coin to see who would go first (I won, naturally), I hiked up my dress, pulled down my G-string, and shoved his face into my crotch. Poor thing almost had an eye poked out by my pube stubble. With his good eye, he took one look at my nine o'clock shadow and said, "That is so not kosher." He stormed out of the back seat and back into the party. Luckily the bar mitzvah boy went with a pirate theme, so my cuz was able to hide his sex injury under an eye patch.

Family get-togethers have been really awkward ever since.

What to pack in your ho-kit:
Condoms
Anal Eaze
Phone charger
Money for a cab
Single-use toothbrush
Pocket rocket
Clean thong
Baby wipes
Mini flashlight to check for STDs

HOW TO BEHAVE
IF YOU
FORGET TO SHAVE

There are some times when no matter how well prepared you are for fucking, you just can't get to your razor/waxer/laser technician in time. For instance, you might have met a hot Aussie dude who wants to punch your mile-high card during the fifteen-hour flight to Sydney, but you're sporting the five o'clock bush shadow. Or perhaps a level-three hurricane has forced your waxer to evacuate the day of your latest lust's hurricane party where you expect to be shut in with him for three days. Here's how to fake it until you make it:

- Do it doggie style: If he's banging you from behind, his dick will come in contact with a smaller pube surface area. And if it accidentally slips into your asshole, that's okay too, since there's generally less hair there.

- Keep your pants on: Tell him you think sometimes it's sexier with your clothes on and only pull your jeans down far enough to get his dick inside your vag. He may think the rough pubes tickling the sides of his peen are your zipper.

- Steer him toward a quickie: Perhaps if the sex is short and frenzied enough, he won't notice that he's got rug burn on his balls.

THE ONLY REASON YOU SHOULD BE IN BED IN THE MIDDLE OF THE DAY IS IF THERE'S A MAN IN IT

I don't really get napping. Unless you're an infant or have passed out from daytime drinking, the only reason you should be in the bed in the middle of the day is if there's a guy in it.

I've got plenty of shit to do during the day: clean the sex stains out of my sheets, cyber-stalk my latest crush, or shop for a new slut-top. I don't have time to take a disco nap.

The last time I went down for a power nap, I woke up to see my then-boyfriend jacking it to his ex on iChat. After I kicked him to the curb (and cleaned the jizz off my keys), I vowed never to be caught napping again. Life's too fucking short. It is totally acceptable, however, to spend the entire day in bed if you're getting stuck good* by a hot guy.

When I was visiting a friend on the East Coast, I was surprised to find that her roommate was a super-sexy dirty hot guy. I was even more surprised to find out that they had never done it. I respected the five-second rule and waited about that long to see if she had any intentions of becoming his bedmate. But it was obvious to me that if she was going to pounce on that dick, she would have done it by now. And since the Depraved Girl code dictates dicks before chicks, I knew she'd have no problem with me making my move.

It was a particularly blustery weekend, so we decided to forgo trying to freeze our tits and asses off to head out to a bar and stayed in with her hot roomie and a bottle of whiskey. Once we were good and drunk, I suggested a game of Truth or Dare. They were both down, so I started off the game by daring the roomie to make out with me. Well, I macked on him so hard that we pretty much had to end it right there because my girl got sick of watching our tongues fuck.

We moved into his bedroom where we had the kind of winter sex that leaves the windows all steamy. You don't get to have that kind of sex in LA. Even though it was cold outside, he kept telling me how fucking hot I was. Little did he know that compliments trigger some sort of blow job reflex in me, so every time he said it I immediately started to give him a hummer, which is usually just foreplay. We did it several more times that night, and in the morning we woke to see the snow drifts had practically reached the sills. So instead of the shopping trip I had planned with my girl, me and the roomie decided to take a snow day and stay in his bed fucking all day.

DEPRA**V**ED fact

Overfucking is one of the leading causes of groin sprains in Germany.

That night was my last night in town and my friend wanted to go out. She got all dressed and ready in her best dress-to-get-laid outfit, but I was still warm and cozy in her roomie's bed and didn't want to leave it. Plus, we were still on our marathon fuck fest, and it was hard for me to even get my mouth free from his dick to tell her I was staying in. I could tell my friend was kind of pissed but I was drunk on cock and not really in the mood to deal.

She went out alone and when she came back, we could hear her drunkenly stumble around the apartment in between our moans. "You're so fucking hot," he told me again, and that must have pushed her over the edge because we heard the front door open and then slam shut. The next thing I knew, she threw open the door to his room. "Here, since you're so fucking hot I thought I'd cool you down," she said as she threw a huge bucket of snow onto our naked bodies. She then locked herself into the only bathroom and took a nice long shower, using up all the hot water as we shivered in his room.

When I returned home, I spent the next three days in bed with a horrible fever. I was "so fucking hot" that my sweat soaked the sheets. I guess there IS another reason to be in bed in the middle of the day: if you overfuck your friend's roommate and her drunken revenge leaves you with a nasty cold. Or if you just have a nasty cold.

IT MAY BE MARC JACOBS, BUT IF IT DOESN'T SHOW OFF YOUR LEGS OR TITS, IT'S WORTHLESS

Now I'm not suggesting you go out there, rock a *Pretty Woman*–style whore dress showing off both your tittays AND your legs, but if you're on the prowl, don't dress for other women, dress to get laid.

Sure, that new Marc Jacobs top you just bought at Barney's is the envy of all those whiny bitches at the office, but if you think you can wear a high-necked button-up top with a pair of jeans out to the bars and get the attention of those dirty hot boys you can't resist, you just wasted a couple of hundred bucks. You don't even have to have big breastacles;* men just can't resist the sight of some bare boob skin.

Of course if you do want to be a man repeller on top, make sure your bottom screams three-dollar ho. I rarely wear a skirt, but when I do, it's short as shit. And when I walk into the bar/club/work wearing my ob/gyn special, I know all the guys are thinking about ripping off those measly ten and a half inches. I'm not saying you can't get laid if you're wearing a burka (or the Western equivalent), but it certainly makes it more of a challenge.

In fact, I once made the mistake of ignoring this cardinal rule one Halloween. Since October 31 is the one night even good girls dress like sluts, as a full-time slut I decided wearing a slutty costume wouldn't be much of a costume at all—it would be more like a regular Tuesday night. So I decided to go classy. And by "classy," I mean I paired this black, shapeless long-sleeved floor-length vintage Gaultier dress with a nun's wimple, and then put my wrists in handcuffs while clutching little girls' panties to go as a "naughty nun." Meanwhile, my frenemy Z was dressed like a sexy cat. Or a sexy cop, or anything stupid that had the word "sexy" in front of it. We had both been crushing on the same guy for a while and he happened to show up at the party we were at.

She took one look at my costume and thought she had a lock on the competish. But she didn't know who the fuck she was dealing with. We both pounced on the poor guy and only left his side during a bathroom truce. (I had drunk five vodka sodas and she had a small bladder, so we decided to go at the same time in order to avoid pissing ourselves.)

As the party wore on, her skirt started heading north as her already flimsy top started heading south. But my witty banter and cock-sucking pout could only go so far. He couldn't take his eyes off her tits and her half-exposed ass-cheek. And I couldn't tear a cleavage hole in the dress or cut the hem to a hooker-length since it was, after all, vintage Gaultier and it had to go back. I had to re-sort to desperate measures. So just when it seemed that he was about to go home with Z, I called a Hail Mary: I whipped off one of my loose handcuffs and slapped it on his wrist.

"Very funny," said Z. "C'mon, where's the key to uncuff him?"

"I stuck it up my vag when we went to the bathroom," I told

her. "You're welcome to look for it, but I think he'd probably prefer to retrieve it himself."

The truth is, by that point, the guy was so drunk he didn't know what had just happened, which made it all the easier for me to lead him out to my car and into my bed.

That was an extreme case, but if you find yourself heading straight to the bars after work and unable to change out of your Armani businesswomen's special, you could always just do what my friend L used to do. She rarely had time to change out of her power suit after a day at the law firm, so if she spotted a guy at the bar who she thought was cute, she'd just walk up to him and say, "I'm not wearing panties." Worked like a charm every time!

DRESS TO GET LAID	
Labels That Help You Get Laid	**Labels That Are Man Repellers**
Bebe	Marc Jacobs
Forever 21	Proenza Schouler
Betsey Johnson	Elizabeth and James
Dolce & Gabbana	3.1 Phillip Lim
Herve Leger	Tory Burch
Victoria's Secret	Banana Republic
Guess	Theory

EVEN
THE UGLY
ONES
CHEAT

After months, years, or even decades of getting fucked over by hot dicks, it's easy to want to give up and settle down for an ugly guy. You might be sick of the hunt, and an ugly guy is just so . . . grateful.

But don't. Because even the ugly ones cheat. Sometimes even more so because they're so used to getting shot down that if the opportunity presents itself to have sex, they'll take it quicker than Lindsay Lohan will snort a line of coke.

Sure, an ugly guy will suck you in with frequent texts and phone calls, expensive dinners and gifts, and cunnilingus that lasts for hours. It's so refreshing to be with a guy who actually wants to be seen with you in the daytime that you convince yourself you can ignore the busted grille, the acne, backne, and chestne, or the fact that YOU normally wouldn't want to be seen with HIM in the daytime if you weren't so tired/desperate/horny. But resist. 'Cause whether you date the hot dick or the ugly guy, either way you're gonna get screwed, so you might as well stick to the type you know, love, and hate.

A few years ago, I got sick of dating all those dirty hot guys who always turned out to be cheating douchebags. So I decided to give the ugly guy with the good job and average car a chance.

At first, his constant attention and adoration annoyed me. Because you never want to be part of a club that would have you as a member (unless it's a swingers' club), I thought it was just pathetic and sad. But I was between jobs and I'd rather eat out at Mastro's than McDonald's, so eventually he wore me down.

Pretty soon, I got used to being treated like a princess. I actually felt myself relaxing in a relationship for the first time, instead of worrying about when the other shoe was gonna drop. I may have had to have sex in the dark while picturing my ex, but at least I could let my Xanax prescription lapse.

After three months, he convinced me to move in with him. He had a great two-bedroom in Hancock Park and said I'd only have to pay my share of the utilities, so I thought why the hell not? After three months and three weeks, I came home one night to find him having butt sex with our Ukrainian neighbor.

I was as shocked as the Ukrainian must have been the first time she saw his flabby ass naked. But strangely, I didn't scream, cry, or even try to key his car like I might have with ex-boyfriends in the past. I simply shut the door, grabbed his car keys, and threw them over the fence as I walked out the front door.

Sometimes you just can't avoid hooking up with an ugly guy, but that doesn't mean you should date him. So you might as well continue dating the dirty hot douches. They go better with the new Balenciaga bag you got from the ugly dude before you dumped his ass!

HOW TO FUCK AN UGLY GUY

It's been three months since you got laid and you're so horny you've worn out the batteries in your vibe. You're at the bar, wasted on one too many whiskey sodas, thanks to Rule #3 and the loser who's been buying you free drink after free drink, hoping the next one may be the golden ticket into your pants.

The more you drink, the hornier you get, but no amount of alcohol is going to change the fact that this loser is straight-up ugly. So how do you get off without getting sick at the sight of his O face?

• Beauty is just a light switch away. Do yourself a favor and keep it in the dark. If you barf up all those free drinks, it's a waste of a buzz.

• Pick a position where the only skin-on-skin contact is penis-to-vagina. There's no reason you have to hold on to his fat rolls or brush against his backne. Try doggie style or reverse cowgirl, making sure all hands are being kept to themselves.

• Keep all clothes ON. You don't need to know what he's hiding under his shirt. Just whip it out of his pants and try not to get your pubes caught on the zipper. Plus, if you keep yours on as well, you won't have to worry about big roaming furry paws to take you out of the moment. (Works best if you're wearing a dress.)

• Absolutely no talking. Unless he can do a convincing Scottish accent that allows you to imagine you're being eaten out by Gerard Butler, place a gag order on the guy.

• Remember: ugly guys work harder, so don't be afraid to lie back and let him do all the work!

IT'S NOT STALKING IF HE SAYS WHERE HE'S GOING TO BE

We've all been guilty of the drive-by. But when desperate bitches everywhere started getting arrested under the anti-stalking laws, we realized we could no longer linger outside his house, cubicle, marijuana dispensary, or anywhere he frequented with impunity.

Luckily, thanks to Facebook and Twitter, we no longer have to.

Now I prefer old-fashioned fuckery* myself (like bribing his friends with drinks and drugs to tell you where he's going to be that night), but this IS the 2000s, and everyone broadcasts their every thought, feeling, and trip to the shitter on their status up-dates these days, so you might as well take advantage.

My friend M took full advantage. She was a master lurker. She friended every guy she ever met, whether she was interested or not, just in case she needed to know his (or his hot friends') whereabouts.

She once stayed up a full forty-eight hours on a nearly lethal combination of Red Bull, Ritalin, and gummy bears, lurking her latest obsession, trying to find out where she could run into him that weekend. When she noticed all of his guy friends were planning on meeting up at the same party, she put on her finest dress-to-get-laid mini and her fuck-me stilettos and showed up at the party. Turns out the raging party she thought she was crashing was their fantasy football draft party.

Now, if you've ever been to one of these nerd fests, you know that shit can take all night. A lesser woman might have turned around and gone home, but a Depraved Girl follows Rule #2: be the last woman standing. Of course, M was the only woman, but while she knows how to compete with hos, competing for a guy's attention with a bunch of fake football teams is a whole 'nother game. But luckily, the Ritalin coursing through her veins helped her to recall every single conversation about football she'd ever pretended to be interested in for the sake of a fuck, so she was able to impress her target with stats and suggestions.

But M made one critical error. Thanks to the Ritalin, she had the worst speed jaw, and with no gummies in sight, she started munching on nuts (peanuts, not testicles). So eventually, around three in the morning, she was forced to leave her guy's side to hit the head. By the time she was finished, her guy had hitched a ride home with a friend, leaving her alone with the skeezy captain of the fantasy football league.

They got to talking and she realized that he had a crush on one of her friends, so they made a pact to trade information on each other's targets. Dangling a hot friend in front of a desperate man will yield you more results than a wiretap, so her hottie never understood how she was always showing up at his coffee shop, outside his office, or even on his dates. When she showed up to his colonoscopy, he knew something was up. He even threatened to call the cops and have her arrested for stalking, but she simply said it wasn't stalking since he'd been broadcasting his every move on Twitter.

"What the fuck are you talking about?" he asked. Unbeknownst to him, his good pal had enabled the GPS on his Twitter feed, so every time he tweeted from his phone, his location appeared.

She didn't get arrested . . . but she didn't get the guy either. She spent so much time going tit for tat with his skeezy pal that she eventually began to see him as a kindred spirit and decided to show him her tits. They've been together ever since.

IS THIS STALKING?

1. You track him down after he posts his whereabouts on Facebook, Twitter, and Foursquare.
   a) Stalking
   b) Not stalking

2. You root through his trash.
   a) Stalking
   b) Not stalking

3. You hack his phone.
   a) Stalking
   b) Not stalking

4. You show up to a party after overhearing him talk about it at a bar.

   a) Stalking

   b) Not stalking

5. You do a drive-by past his house.

   a) Stalking

   b) Not stalking

6. You camp outside his window for forty-eight hours without moving and peeing in jars.

   a) Stalking

   b) Not stalking

Answers: 1. b, 2. a, 3. a, 4. b, 5. b, 6. a

ALWAYS SUPPORT YOUR GIRLS

One of the most important rules in the Depraved Girl's code is that you've got to blindly follow your girlfriends into battle, even if they're on a suicide mission.

Now this rule could apply to something as simple as going on a stalkapalooza of her latest lust's favorite bars and clubs all weekend (been there), or holding up your drunken friend as she takes a piss squat in the alley behind the crowded club so she doesn't get pee on her new platform pumps (definitely been there).

Even if it's late Sunday night and you've got a two-day hangover, if she gets a tip that the dirty hot dick is at the Short Stop, you tear yourself away from *True Blood* and your second bottle of wine and you go. Even if he's a cheat who's broken her heart time and time again, you slap a smile and a couple of extra pounds of concealer on your face, pop a Ritalin, and do everything you can to help her get what she wants, even if what she wants is bad for her.

I once found myself in this exact situation with my girlfriend C. She had a huge thing for a guy I wouldn't fuck even if he roofied me, but C had a taste for men with slight BO and a biting tongue, and who am I to stand in the way of a Depraved Girl and her latest lust? Besides, she offered to buy my drinks in exchange for my assistance, and fuck, you know how I feel about free drinks.

We stalked the stinky bastard—who was taking the dirty hot thing a bit too far by choosing not to shower for days—over a five-day period and finally met up with him on a Monday night at a bar in East Hollywood. He spent the evening making snarky comments to my girl until she had plied him with enough whiskey sodas that he was too drunk to be droll (and me with enough that I actually started to think he might deserve my friend's vag).

That's when she pulled her classic move on him: she said we should head to this hot new underground bar downtown, the kind you needed a password to get into, knowing full well that the bar was closed. But since she also offered to drive, he'd be trapped and she'd end up taking him home.

We piled into her car, them in front and me in the back seat. As her target rambled on about some pretentious new indie band that had recently "sold out" when they started actually selling albums, my friend, who had had plenty of whiskey sodas of her own, lost control of the car while attempting to shift his stick and hit a telephone pole.

As soon as we confirmed that none of us were hurt, we got out of the car to survey the damage. That's when two cop cars rolled up.

"Which one of you was driving?" they asked. I looked over at my girl's distraught face and I couldn't tell what she was more afraid of: getting arrested or losing out at what could be her one opportunity to bone the boy.

"I was," I said, before she could respond, hoping that she'd still be able to salvage the booty. Besides, I was confident that the whiskey had worn off enough that I would be able to blow a legal number into the breathalyzer. Because after I blow something, things usually go my way.

Shit, was I wrong.

I blew a .12. They cuffed me and put me in back of one cop car, while they took C and her dude to the station in another where they said they'd be able to call someone for a ride or catch a cab.

I spent the next several hours cuffed to a bench inside the Hollywood police station next to a famous actor who had been arrested for snorting coke off two groupies' tits while attempting to drive down Sunset Boulevard (and no, it wasn't Charlie Sheen; this guy has a way better publicist). He and I got to talking, mostly about what drug combos we adored—Xannies and a martini for me, coke and X for him.

They would have released me, but I was pretty belligerent all night and they wouldn't let me go until I could get a "responsible adult" to come get me. The only person I knew who would have been sober at that hour was my pregnant sister and the bitch wasn't answering her phone.

At about four a.m., just as my celeb friend's manager had posted his bail, my girl C showed up to take me home.

"What the fuck are you doing here?" I asked. "Shouldn't you be at home getting a finger up the ass?"

C explained that her crush, who turned out to be the worst kind of dick, grabbed the first cab home from the police station—alone. She had spent the night sobering up at Roscoe's Chicken and Waffles and getting her car out of the impound instead of getting pounded. I couldn't believe I took a DUI rap all for nothing—no sixty-nine, no fucking, no anal—nothing!

The celeb came to say goodbye to me, and C almost shit her pants. She had loved him since his first gig on that show and had seen every single one of his movies, even the one he got fat for. Her vagina immediately started to tingle out of muscle memory because she used to masturbate to him every night for a year.

I was tired, I was sweaty, and I was coming down from my contact high off the fumes being emitted from the celeb all night.

I just wanted to go home, but my efforts to get C laid couldn't go to waste, so I told C to leave me there and go bang my new pal in the back of the Town Car his manager sent for him before he left.

My next bench mate wasn't quite as entertaining. And sitting next to the alcoholic dumpster diver for the next forty-five minutes as my friend did her thang made me want to burn my clothes. When she finally got me home, I threw my clothes in the trash and rubbed the stank off my skin. Then she treated me to a Champagne brunch at the Four Seasons, a whole new outfit at Barney's, and an attorney who got me off on the DUI charges.

As I've said before, a good fuck is hard to find, so if your pal has the chance to get some, you should be happy for her vagina instead of pissed that she's ditching you. After all, she'll be there to do it for you when the situation is reversed.

HOW TO FUCK
A CELEBRITY

You can't swing a vagina in LA without meeting some celebrity who's got such low standards that he'll fuck anything that moves. So as a result, my girlfriends and I have seen more celebrity dick than a tranny hooker.

But I'm realizing sexing a celeb isn't just an LA thing. In fact, there's horny celebs all over the world who are just dying to validate their egos by screwing us mere mortals. So I've put together a few tips to help you get on, get off, and get over it if you ever find yourself in a similar situation:

• Fuck him. Do it for the story you'll tell your girlfriends, who will be living vicariously through every thrust. You owe it to them.

- Do NOT try to date him! In fact, try never to talk to him again. A celebrity is by definition the most overconfident insecure person you'll ever meet. They expect you to adore them. So after you drive him mad in bed, don't ever respond to him again, and you'll drive him mad in another way.

- Whatever you do, don't make a sex tape. Sure, these days, for an actor, it's akin to winning an Oscar, but you'll just be "that girl who made a sex tape with David Spade." Where can you go from there? Nowhere—except porn.

Fucking a celebrity is something every girl should do if she has the chance, but if you are going to get freaky with the famous, DEFINITELY practice uber-safe sex. There is a very good possibility you'll only be two degrees or so away from some starlet with a bad case of the herp.

THERE'S MORE THAN ONE WAY TO FUCK A MAN

Although there are all kinds of ways to screw a guy in bed, the fucking I'm talking about has to do with his head. That's right, girls. I'm talking revenge.

Let's say you've been dating this guy who is so your type (full sleeve of tats, vintage car) for about two months. You've been inseparable since the night you dragged him back to your place after bingeing on tequila at the Snakepit. It's getting serious enough to finally have "the talk"—you know, where you agree that it's okay to fart in front of each other.

Everything seems to be heading toward a happily ever after, but then he starts getting cagey. He won't be seen with you in the daytime anymore and when you try to push his head down toward your crotch during a late-night booty call, he resists. After a little investigation, you find out HE'S HAD A GIRLFRIEND THE ENTIRE TIME! She just happened to be out of town when you two first hooked up.

So do you sit around crying to your girlfriends while watching *Bridget Jones's Diary* on a loop? Or do you make HIM cry? Obviously, I vote for the latter.

Fuck his car: A D-bag loves nothing more than his car, so hit him in his figurative balls. You could go the Carrie Underwood route and key the paint, smash the headlights with a baseball bat, and slash all his tires, OR you could do some real damage. Some say it's a myth, but a friend of mine swears (from experience) that pouring sugar in a gas tank will fuck up the engine. Powdered sugar, sand, and bleach will also mess that shit up. Now I'm not condoning this, as it IS illegal, so if you do this, make sure you're ready for the consequences.

Fuck his Facebook: Wait until you know he'll be out at some loud club for the night and then have a really, really great friend leave this post on his wall. Then wait for the comments from his girlfriend and other hos to roll in.

 Dominic Murphy
Guinness for lunch and whiskey for dinner.
Like • Comment • 2 minutes ago

 4 people like this.

 Becky Rhoder Thanks for giving me herpes, asshole!
about 1 minute ago • Like

Julia Dexter WHAT???!!
about 1 minute ago • Like

Write a comment. . .

Fuck his home: The idiot is too stupid to remember that he told you where he keeps the hide-a-key. Use it to get in and then piss in his laundry detergent, or if you're really committed, move (or re-move) one item every week until he thinks he's going crazy.

Fuck his best friend: There's nothing a guy hates more than the idea of his best friend's dick going in (and out of) something he considered his. Now there are some guys who won't want to violate the "bro code" and stay far away from vaginas previously penetrated by their BFF, but that's nothing a little roofie colada couldn't cure.

Hopefully you're totally aware that some of these tactics are entirely illegal, so proceed at your own risk. And if you do decide to follow some of my suggestions, take a sweater. Jail is cold.

SETTLING
IS FOR
QUITTERS

Have you ever been so tired of getting your heart ripped out by guy after dirty hot guy that the dirty bum on the corner who keeps asking you out is starting to look like a good option for you? Well don't. Because settling is for quitters.

One of my formerly depraved girlfriends, A, found herself so tired of her dirty hot boyfriends pulling down their pants and taking a dump on her heart that she decided she was going to pack up her snatch and settle for the next "nice guy" who asked her out.

Four months later, I found myself at her wedding eating filet mignon and wondering aloud to my friend V why no one was mentioning that our girl's special guy was so special that he had a hard time tying his shoes. He was seriously dumb as a box of rocks. And that's an insult to rocks. But A seemed so deliriously happy that she was virtually unrecognizable as the girl who only a short year before had to complete anger management counseling after she tried to set her cheating ex-boyfriend's new girlfriend's hair on fire. But you'd have to be delirious to marry a guy whose idea of intellectual stimulation was watching *Wheel of Fortune*.

But after the toasts, after the first dance, and after the cutting of the cake, even my cold black heart began to melt just a little bit. But V had been sold on the whole thing. She even started to cry after they took off in their "just married" short bus. "I want that," V said.

So the very next day, V set out to find her own stupid guy. V always was a competitive bitch, so she somehow managed to outdo A with a guy who didn't just have the IQ of an inbred, but may have actually been one. But V had gotten a glimpse of what a non-fucked-up relationship was like and wanted a chance at her own happily ever after—and she was convinced that she would get it with this idiot. I guess she thought the lower his IQ, the less likely he'd be to cheat on her.

One night she came home early from work and decided she'd surprise her new man with a little P&P: Popeye's fried chicken (his favorite) and poon—his idea of an amazing Friday night. But when she got there, she realized he had already started without her on the poon part—he was fucking another girl who looked like she just escaped from an institution. V later

told me that she wasn't so upset with the fact that he was cheating on her, but that he was doing it with such a fucking dog.

She vowed never to settle again, and since that day has only allowed herself to get fucked over by the hot ones.

There are no guarantees that after you and your idiot get married, have sex (with the lights off of course), and pop out a couple of little dummies he won't straight up leave your cellulite-ridden mom-ass for his secretary in ten years. All men cheat, even the ugly ones (Rule #15), so you may as well spend your prime fucking years getting screwed by hot guys. They'll all screw you over in the end anyway, so at least you can give yourself good spank material for those rare nights when you are alone.

IF YOU TRAVEL MORE THAN TWENTY MILES FOR A BOOTY CALL, AT LEAST ONE OF YOU MUST GET OFF

These days, a trick will travel to another continent just for some good dick. Hell, we'll even go to another area code just for some so-so sex. And if you do take the trouble to get your ass off your couch and away from your bottle of red wine and bad reality TV to drive over half an hour away to get some, then there really should be some type of orgasm had, if not by all, then at least by one.

Several years ago, I met this guy at a party. He was wearing long sleeves in August, but he was cute, funny, and straight, so I gave him my number.

A few nights later he booty-called me at eleven p.m. "Come over," he said. "I wanna fuck you so hard you'll forget your own name."

"I'm leaving now," I said, pulling on my ankle boots. "Where do you live?"

"Northridge."

The Valley??? Asshole tricked me with a 323 area code! But I was horny, and I was ready to go, so I got in my car and made the twenty-mile trek from Hollywood.

I got there around midnight and the minute I walked through the door, he immediately grabbed me, pushed me up against the wall, and started macking on me. I noticed that once again he was wearing long sleeves, but I was distracted by his tongue drifting downward. I was naked before I knew it, but he was still fully clothed, so I reached for his shirt, pulled it over his head, and revealed the FURRIEST CHEST I'D EVER SEEN!

Now, I'm not opposed to a little chest hair (it's actually quite sexy on some guys), but this guy was covered neck to wrist in a thick pelt. Taking off his shirt was like opening a can of Pillsbury Crescent Rolls; you hear a pop and then all this hair just explodes out of its container.

It dried me up quicker than Accutane. Seriously, I was completely turned off. I was tempted to leave right then and there. But I had driven all that way . . . so I let him eat me out and then I bolted.

Now body hair isn't necessarily a deal breaker for me, it's more of a deal bender. But here are several valid reasons for pulling out of a verbal or implied agreement to knock boots.

• **He has a micro-dick*:** If his peen is smaller than your thumb, than all bets are off.

• **He doesn't know how to eat the puss:** If you're in stage-three foreplay and the guy goes down like a dog licking peanut butter (i.e., sloppy and all over the place), it may be a preview of what he's gonna do with his peen. It's totally acceptable to get the fuck out of there before you spend the night having bad sex when your perfectly orgasmic vibrator is waiting for you at home.

- **You found someone more fuckable:** Let's face it, Cuntinis,* we ARE women and we like to change our mind a gazillion times about what pair of shoes we're wearing out, and those just go on our feet. If you found someone more fuckable in the time the booty call went out, then by all means, cancel the contract and make a new agreement.

HOW FAR SHOULD YOU TRAVEL TO GET OFF?

50 miles: You both get off.

Leave the country: You see Jesus, Mary, and Joseph having an orgy in the manger.

20 miles: Someone comes.

Leave the state: You see Jesus.

HOW TO TELL IF A GUY WILL BE GOOD AT GOING DOWN

There are some times when you're single and horny, and your vibe just won't do. You want satisfaction but just can't handle the thought of dealing with a new guy's dick cheese. Cunnilingus is your only answer.

But how can you tell that some guy you just met will be good at going down? Guys have the DSL* indicator, but what have we girls got?

Well, you're in luck my horny whores, because I've put together a list of telltale signs that may clue you in to an expert vag snacker:

- He orders his ice cream in a cone instead of a cup. Clearly, this guy likes to lick.

- He's metrosexual. If a guy spends three hours on his hair, imagine how much time he'll spend down there!

- He's a slow driver. If he's a guy who isn't afraid to stop and take his cues from others, chances are he'll be good at following orders.

- He's overweight. Guys with food issues take their eating out very seriously.

- It takes him more than three licks to get to the center of a Tootsie Pop. Just think how long he'll take getting to your gooey center!

- Tell him he has something on his eyebrow. If he licks it off, you're good to go.

IT'S NOT ABOUT HOW YOU GET HIS ATTENTION, IT'S ABOUT HOW YOU KEEP IT

There are all sorts of depraved ways to get a guy's attention, starting with grabbing his ass. Hell, grab his cock. I have one friend who liked to "oopsie" spill her drink on guys she wanted to bang. It doesn't really matter how you meet; it's what you do with his meat afterward that'll have him crying for more.

For instance, my friend O would "accidentally" spill her drink on a guy. Then she started to get more aggressive. She decided that she was going to start *throwing* drinks on guys, in what she'd later explain as a huge misunderstanding. She'd make up some story about how she thought he was the guy who fucked his girlfriend's thirteen-year-old sister at her bat mitzvah. He'd usually be so outraged by the pedophilia aspect that they'd end up in intense conversation all night . . . that led to intense fucking all night.

After she had him, that slut would pull out every trick in her slag-bag to keep his attention by doing everything from role-play to threesomes. Once she even tried to learn how to shoot ping-pongs out of her hoo-hah.

So after about three months of her fuckstravaganza,* she would get pretty tired and pick a fight (that usually involved throwing a drink on her man) just so she could give her vag a break and nurse her bangover. Then she'd start the process all over again.

But kinky sex isn't the only way you can keep a man's attention. Another cray cray* friend of mine, F, would do some real fucked-up shit to keep her man interested. Like every time she felt her man's attention waning, she would "steal" his cat. She'd wait until she knew he was out, then take the pussy and hide it in her house.

He'd be so distraught over his missing pet that F would swoop in and play the hero, creating "Missing Cat" posters, driving the streets at night, and reaching out to all the neighbors to see if anyone had seen his poor little kitty. She'd insist on spending every night with him, comforting him with a hot meal and an even hotter fuck. After enough time had passed and she felt they had sufficiently reconnected on an emotional and sexual level, she would miraculously turn up with the cat after receiving a call about one of her posters.

This happened about three times in four months, and her dude never suspected a thing. But after every cat nabbing, their honeymoon period would get shorter and shorter, so F had to step up the pussy grabbing. One night her man came home right when she was in the midst of one of her missions. She had the cat in her arms when she heard the key turn in the door. She panicked and jumped out the window onto the fire escape, the cat still in her arms. When the kitty saw her owner, she started mewing like crazy. F tried to put her hand over the cat's mouth but it was too late; he heard what was going on. He opened the window to see F standing out there with the cat.

"What the fuck are you doing?" he asked. She tried to explain that the cat had escaped yet again and she had just found it on the fire escape, but as dumb as this guy was, he finally put two and two together and kicked her to the curb.

After that, she stuck to less criminal ways of keeping a guy's attention—like home-cooked meals at night and blow jobs for breakfast.

HAVE VACATION SEX AT HOME

I love having vacation sex because there are absolutely no consequences. You don't have to be embarrassed if you queef, and there's no danger he'll come after you when he finds out that you're not really the daughter of the Miami Dolphins' owner and there are no box seats waiting for him at will call.

So how can you take advantage of being able to fuck with impunity while you're at home?

• **Find a tourist dude in your hometown:** If you live in a larger city, chances are there's a hostel nearby with horny Euro tourists. Hang out at the nearest bar and pretend to have an overwhelming fascination with whatever country they came from. Even if you know nothing about Belgium, you can get away with pretending by blaming it on their poor English skills.

Example:

> You: "Omigod, I've always wanted to go to Copenhagen!"
> Him: "You mean Brussels?"
> You: "Yes, that's what I said. Are you sure you speak perfect English?"

Hooking up with one of these guys is like shooting fish in a barrel. The only things you have to watch out for are the other predators swarming around waiting to get a taste of some continental ass. But Depraved Girls don't go down without a fight. Well, they do go down, but only with their hookups.

• **Pretend to be a tourist in your hometown:** If you live in a teeny-tiny place, this probably won't work (although you could just jump into your pickup and head a few towns over), but for those of you who aren't cousin-fuckers, it's time to pull out those junior high school drama skills and put on an act.

I recommend heading to the nearest Irish pub (there's one in every city) with a tourist book or a map of your town. If no drunk dude approaches you offering to help you find something, you have the perfect opener: "Can you tell me how to get to [insert hometown landmark here]?" Actually, the perfect opener is, "I'm only in town for one night and I want to fuck," but some girls love a little verbal foreplay.

If you plan on going with option no. 2 and you're bringing along a girlfriend, make sure you get your stories straight ahead of time. Don't make it too elaborate; after your fourth whiskey soda, you'll have forgotten what foreign accent you're supposed to be speaking in and she'll have forgotten her panties at the previous bar. Your targets may not drive you back to pick them up if they find out you aren't really part of an international burlesque troupe touring the U.S. and looking for local men to act as a kind of "focus group" to help you hone your act.

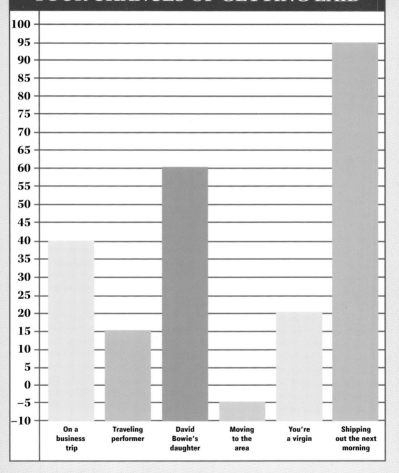

A PITY FUCK DOESN'T HAVE TO BE PITIFUL

There ain't no shame in getting laid, whether your partner is fucking you out of pity or not.

Once I had to tell this guy I was totally creaming for (but who was surprisingly reluctant to bone me) that my father had died . . . the same weekend my dog ran away . . . and I got laid off from work. "I just really need a stiff drink and a good friend right now," I told him, guilting him into going out with me.

Well, a lot of beers and a few fake tears later, I took him home and got him to comfort me on my couch. As his hand rubbed my shoulder, I grabbed it and moved it south. Like way south, so he was rubbing my vag. "I don't know about this," he tried to protest, but by then, MY hand was on his crotch, so it was only a matter of time before he stopped thinking with his head (that head, anyway).

The sex was amaze. He was all trying to be gentle, you know, 'cause I was "in mourning," but that just meant I could position him any way I wanted to and he couldn't say no. Of course, in the morning, my dad called (I still rock an old-school answering machine to live-screen my calls), so for a split second it was a bit awkward, until I told him my ex-boyfriend liked to call himself "daddy." Sure, he fucked me out of pity, but at least I got laid, so what's the pity in that?

And if you're the one administering the pity fuck, lucky you.

It's your good deed for the year, so you can forget about having to visit grandma at the nursing hospital!

In my early twenties, I was working as a cocktail waitress at a West Hollywood club. While it was smack in the middle of its ten-minute reign as the hottest club in LA, the hottest bartender in LA came to work there. All the sluts who worked there would've given their left fake tit to fuck him, but for some reason he wanted me. And I didn't even have to do anything to encourage him. Go figure.

One night after the club closed down, we all stuck around at the bar having drinks he was expertly mixing for us. When our boss finally kicked us out, all the other amateur bitches were trying to pretend they were too drunk to drive home and asked the hot bartender to give them a ride. He simply called a cab for each and every one of them and picked my drunk ass up and stuffed me in his car, saying, "You're coming home with me." I didn't argue.

We got back to his place and he tied me up to his bedposts with two of his neckties. I got ready for the fucking of my young life when he unzipped his pants and pulled out a teeny-tiny peen. It was, seriously, the length of my thumb. I had to stifle a laugh. Normally I would chew through my ties and run out, but the look the hot-ass bartender gave me when he saw my almost-reaction was so sad and pitiful that I decided to fuck him anyway. In my drunken state, I couldn't even really feel anything and since I was still tied up and my movement was restricted, I found myself nodding off slightly until he apparently came.

To this day I don't include him in my "number" because I can't be sure his dick ever even entered my vagina.

WHAT EARNS YOU A PITY FUCK

Here's What Happens	Here's What You Get
You get chewed out at work.	You get a pity pat on the back.
Your car gets totaled in an accident.	You get a pity hug.
Your dog goes to the vet.	You get a pity kiss.
Your ex left you for someone richer, smarter, and way better looking than you.	You get a pity finger bang.
You get injured in an accident.	You get pity oral sex.
A family member dies.	Congratulations, you've earned a pity fuck!

NO RULES APPLY TO YOUR BACKUP GUY

If you're already creaming over the thought of some cute guy's cock, any lesser dicks you come into contact with in the meantime are just backup guys. Therefore, absolutely no rules apply.

You can pretty much do and say whatever you want around your backup guy because he's on your B team. There's a possibility you may play him, but only if one of your starters injures his dick. So while you don't want to do anything that will ruin your future chances of fucking (which, let's be honest, when it comes to guys just means gaining weight), you don't have to play any games with him.

After a four-month dry spell, my girl T was finally crushing on some hot young thing. She was doing everything she could to get into his boxer-briefs: lurking his Facebook page, befriending his exes to get the dirt on what he liked, lingering at whatever bar/party/fast food restaurant he was at until she was the last woman standing, but so far, she was still just masturbating to the thought of boning him instead of actually boning him.

One afternoon, she found herself at a beach party she had gone to because someone had given her a tip that he was going to be there. It ended up being a bad tip, but while there, she met a guy who was cute, young, and fuckable. They exchanged numbers.

The next day, she asked me if she should make the first move and text him first.

"Fuck yeah," I said, "he's your backup guy. Text him if you want to text him, ask him out if you want to ask him out, and fuck him if you want to fuck him!"

A backup guy is like a sex savings account. You can make deposits and withdrawals with absolutely no penalties. He's not the one you really want, so you can't lose.

One of my backup guys was a work friend. We used to eat lunch every day in the cafeteria together and talk shit about the stupid ugly people we worked with (which was pretty much everyone but us). He was cute in a Midwestern corn-fed white boy kind of way, which meant that I would fuck him, but only when I exhausted the seemingly endless supply of dirty hot dicks and disenfranchised hipsters that I tended to gravitate toward.

I pretty much had no censor around him. I would talk about the very unsexy reason I initially stopped wearing underwear (ingrown hairs from waxing) to the fact that no matter how many times I explained it to him, my current fuck just could not do this

DEPRAVED fact

Two-thirds of women polled said they don't back up a booty call.

twisty thing with his tongue when he was going down on me that I needed in order to get off. I once even made him check out a suspicious-looking mole on the back of my thigh.

Well, one night the unthinkable happened. I finally found myself all dressed up with no dirty hot guy to lust after. That's when I texted my backup guy and asked him to meet me at my favorite dive bar. I could have just asked him to come back to my place to fuck, but that would have been a waste of a hot outfit.

He met me at the bar and I bought us drinks. (Yes, I bought them because no rules apply, remember?) We proceeded to make fun of all the stupid ugly people at the bar until we were sufficiently drunk. With my whiskey soda breath, I leaned over and told him that we should go back to my place to write embarrassing things on our coworkers' Facebook walls—or to have sex—it was up to him.

Obviously he chose the latter. It wasn't the most amazing sex or anything, but guess what? He totally did that twisty thing with his tongue that got me off.

The next day, I got a text from this hot asshole I had a huge thing for the year earlier. He was back in town and wanted to meet up. I showed the text to my backup guy at lunch and asked if he would call the asshole and give him instructions on the twisty thing. Backup guy never ate lunch with me again, but my hot-ass quota was back up, so I really didn't give a fuck.

DON'T BE AFRAID TO FUCK ON THE FIRST DATE

Conventional dating rules say that you shouldn't have sex with a guy before the third date. But I say, fuck the rules and fuck on the first date if you want to.

You may be holding out because you're worried that he won't respect you if you give in too soon. But if that's the only reason, I'm worried that you're too concerned with what some dick may or may not be thinking and not respecting your own vagina enough to give it what it wants.

If a guy is all about the challenge, he's going to lose interest after you fuck anyway, whether it's on the first date or the third. So why not do it on the first date so that if he does walk away, you don't have anything invested yet? Besides, he may not even stick around for three dates, and then you'll regret not having sex with him on the first date because at least then you'd have gotten laid.

My girlfriend, K, is so fucking patient, she waited a whole year for her perfect motorcycle-riding guy to break up with his imperfect girlfriend. 'Course, she did help things along a bit in the breakup department with the aid of a gallon of mudslides, a hot tub, and the girl's ex-boyfriend, but the very minute his Facebook status changed from "In a Relationship" to "It's Complicated," she called and asked him out for drinks.

"It was the best date of my life," she later told me.

"The sex was hot?" I asked.

"No, we didn't do it," she said.

I practically choked on my Xantini. "What the fuck do you mean? Your vagina waited patiently for a year for this dude and didn't do him?"

"It's the first date," she said. "I'm waiting until the third. I don't want him to think I'm a slut!"

Date no. 2 came but she didn't. Afterward, my girl started getting prepped for the big date no. 3. She waxed, she plucked, she tanned. Hell, she even got her asshole bleached.

The next day, bright and early, I called her up. "So? Is your pussy sore?"

"I don't want to talk about it," she said, sounding depressed.

"What? He had a micro-dick?"

"Worse. He's dead."

Apparently, her bike-riding hottie got into a horrible accident the day of their sex date and his dick was being buried (along with the rest of him) before she'd ever gotten the chance to wrap her cooch around it.

Bottom line is, men all leave one way or another. So why wait for some arbitrary date to get off? Might as well have some fun and get laid while you can!

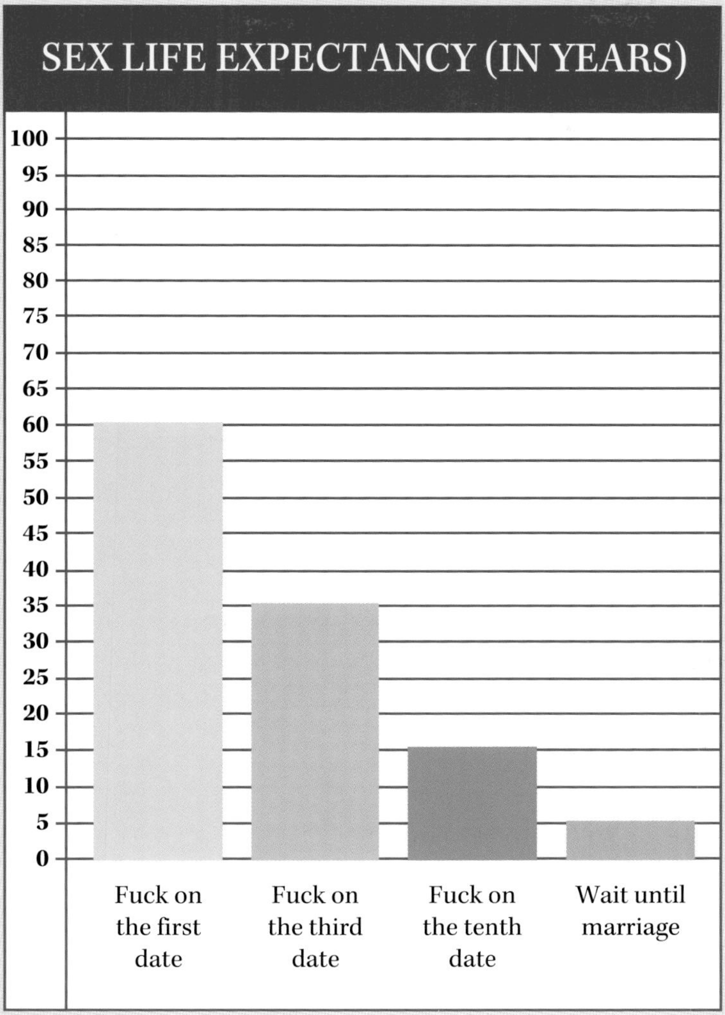
SEX LIFE EXPECTANCY (IN YEARS)
100
95
90
85
80
75
70
65
60
55
50
45
40
35
30
25
20
15
10
5
0
Fuck on the first date
Fuck on the third date
Fuck on the tenth date
Wait until marriage

MEN LOVE THE CHALLENGE OF A TAKEN WOMAN

Just as a Depraved Girl can't resist an unavailable man, guys are equally drawn to women in relationships. But whereas women find something more attractive when it's wanted by someone else, men find a taken woman more attractive not only because she's a challenge, but also because at the end of the night, she goes home to someone else. And there's nothing hotter than expiration-date sex.

My friend M got so much dick when she wore her mother's old wedding ring out that she bought herself a brand-new two-carat princess-cut diamond to wear on her left hand. It's already paid for itself in ass.

One night at the Hotel Café, she started a casual conversation with one of the many disenfranchised hipsters (DH) who were there to check out the local band. He was nonchalant at first, and so was she. Until she nonchalantly flashed her two-carat diamond in his face.

"You're married?" he said, suddenly perking up. Now, being an experienced trick, M knew that in order to close the deal, she couldn't jump in with tales of being trapped in an unhappy relationship because that would make her seem like easy pickings and eliminate the challenge aspect.

So instead, she told the DH how much she missed her huz, who was away on a work trip, and how hard it was to sleep in the bed without him, especially since they usually fucked at least three times a night.

As one band played into the next, and they downed more and more bourbon and waters together, M went in for the kill: she started playing the "reluctant flirt," with lots of "I shouldn't be doing this" and "this is so bad," and the next thing she knew, he was coercing her to take a marriage "time-out" and come home with him after the bar closed, just to "talk." Well, obvi, "talk" turned into some of the best sex she'd ever had in her life.

But M made a classic mistake. Instead of running home to wait for her "husband's" morning call from the road, she suggested they spend the weekend together, going to brunch at the Griddle and giving each other hand jobs in the back of the movie theater at the Grove. They were having so much fucking fun (and fun fucking) that each of them played the "what if M was single" game, and lamented the fact that they hadn't met before she was married.

DEPRAVED fact

Fifty percent of marriages end in divorce. The other 50 percent stay together by fucking someone else.

Of course, Sunday night came around, and again, instead of rushing home to greet her returning hubby and starting a fake illicit affair that would entail lots of lunchtime motel sex, she made up some excuse about his plane being delayed until the morning and made plans to spend the night again.

That's when he started getting cagey. "Don't you want to go home and wash me off of you before he gets home?" he asked.

M was high on the great sex so she didn't realize that what she was going to say next would ruin her whole scheme. "Before who gets home?"

"Your husband," he responded.

"Oh, of course," she covered, but she couldn't tell if he was fully convinced.

Over the next few weeks, M just couldn't help herself. She called and texted him on a daily basis, even though he rarely responded. Desperate, M decided to come clean, hoping the reason he wasn't interested was because he was feeling guilty carrying on with a married woman. When she finally got him on the phone, she asked him, "What if I wasn't married?" His answer? "What if you never called me again?"

Whoops!

SOMETIMES
A GIRL
JUST
NEEDS
A GOOD
FUCK

I have this friend, R, who is hot, smart, successful, and totally DTF.* But she can never find a guy who will give it to her good on a regular basis!

You'd think a woman who wanted some NSA sex would be every guy's dream, but instead, her encounters turn out to be a nightmare of missed opportunities. Or the ones she meets who ARE willing to stick it to her good are usually some kind of fetish freaks. Hey, there's nothing wrong with a little spanking, whipping, and role-playing now and then, but she's definitely not into the furries.

Are guys so intimidated by a girl who's totally blunt about the fact that she just wants a good fuck that they can't perform?

She thought she'd found the perfect fuck buddy in this guy D. He was sexy in that beard-growing, mountain-climbing, out-doorsy kind of way and lived in San Diego, just far enough from LA to keep things fresh and exciting, but not so far that you spent more time masturbating to him than fucking him.

They had both just gotten out of long-term relationships and weren't looking for anything serious except a serious fuck. The first few times they hooked up, my friend, who's had a long and illustrious slut career, said he was hands down the most amazing fuck she'd ever had. Like out-of-body experience good. The kind of sex that makes you want to have his abortion.

But after two months of getting boned in either her area code or his on a weekly basis, something weird happened. He started talking to her. At first it was just pillow talk after sex, mostly about his ex and how he wasn't sure if he wanted her back or not. But then he started talking about his dream to move to New York and become a chef. And this was before sex. She indulged his babbling because she knew that after he was done he would stick her good. He started calling her on the phone in between their trysts.

"You're so easy to talk to," he'd say, not knowing that her "uh-huhs" on the other side of the phone were really "uhh—mmms" because she was masturbating to his voice instead of listening. Pretty soon the time between conversations got shorter and shorter, but the time between their fuck fests got longer and longer.

When she DID make the drive down to see him, sometimes he wouldn't want to have sex at all! Despite the fact that she'd do everything in her power to entice him, short of hoovering his dick, he no longer got hard, so sex wouldn't even be an option. In fact, one time, he even suggested they just get in bed, cuddle (ugh!), and talk all night! What kind of bullshit is that, she wanted to know. "I didn't drive my ass down to fucking San Diego to cuddle!" she told me later.

So one weekend she traded a bunch of Xannies to her roommate for some Viagra and showed up at his place with an open bottle of wine she had dosed with the penis pills. "I thought we could chat over a couple of glasses," she said, making sure to pour him a nice big one, hoping his cock would also get nice and big.

He drank the entire bottle on his own. In less than an hour, he was as hard as a sledgehammer. But little did R know that wine made him more emotional than a fourteen-year-old girl on the rag. So instead of crying out with pleasure, he was just crying. Mostly about his ex-girlfriend, his unhappiness in his career, and the dog he lost when he was eight. You know, real arousing shit. But despite his total breakdown, he had a raging hard-on, and he wanted to get rid of it.

It was the first time R was going to have sex with him in months. But she took one look at his tear-stained face and snotty nose and stood up. "I wanna get fucked good, but not this badly," she said. She drove herself home at three a.m., got into bed, and got off with her trusty vibe.

The next day, she placed an ad in Craigslist's Casual Encounters.

Looking for a Good Fuck (w4m)

I'm a girl who's looking for a hard dick, but every man I seem to find is a soft pussy. If you're down for some straight fucking without a side of small talk, then you might be the guy for me. Willing to drive up to twenty miles to get off. Cuddle rapists* need not respond.

DON'T FUCK WHERE YOU DRINK

It's very easy to see why a girl might fall for a bartender. Not only are they usually panty-moisteningly hot, but it's their job to flirt with you and serve you alcohol. Sounds like the perfect guy, right? WRONG!

A Depraved Girl doesn't let anything get between her and her vodka. Trying to get it on with the guy who provides you with your liquid dinners only jeopardizes your relationship with alcohol in the future. And THAT is the relationship you really need to take care of.

I learned this the hard way, when after accepting too many free vodka tonics from T at one of my local bars, I accepted his invitation to go home with him. The sex wasn't that memorable (truthfully, I can't remember much of ANYTHING from that night), but I thought the consummation of our bartender/alcoholic relationship meant free drinks for life!

Well, the next night, after I had stuck a suppository up my ass to stop the puking (yeah, that happened), I headed back to the bar to claim a little hair of the dog—free, of course. I grabbed a bar stool, then grabbed his face, and gave him a big wet kiss. I barely even noticed him recoiling in horror before ordering a bloody Mary.

Well, apparently, T had a GF, and she was big and mean and wasn't afraid to use her man hands to try to issue me a beat-down. Even though I had no idea he even had a girlfriend, and I didn't even start the fight, the owners were her pals, and just like that, I was banned for life.

After years of drinking at the same place, suddenly I had to go find a new watering hole, and this time, I learned to keep my hole firmly shut to bartenders. I guess it helped that my new bartender was gay. . . .

But girls, this rule isn't just for bartenders; it pretty much applies to all "help": Personal trainers, hairstylists, acupuncturists, bank tellers—they'll draw you in with their Axe body spray and the promise of free checking, but trust me, nothing is free!

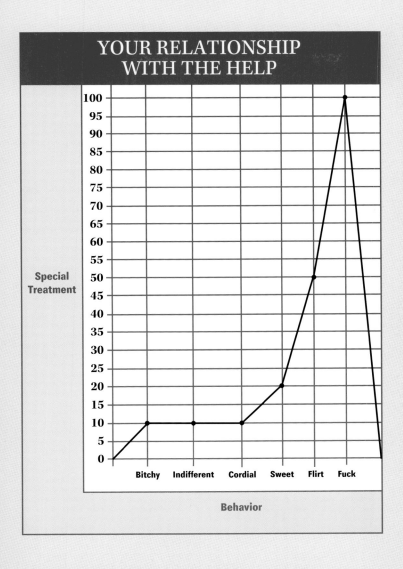

LOVE CAN FADE, BUT HERPES LASTS A LIFETIME

Before you pull on your Frederick's of Hollywood crotchless panties and mix yourself a Xantini in preparation for your weekend stalkapalooza, I thought I'd take a minute to talk to you about what happens after your drunken hookup.

That's right, I'm talking STDs. Before you jump into the sack with the DJ that you've been drooling over for months, ask yourself if his dick is worth contracting the herp.

Now, there's plenty of people who have gone on to lead very successful lives with full-blown STDs (like half of Hollywood and three-quarters of professional athletes), but if you've managed to dodge them thus far in your slut career, you might as well hold out as long as possible.

Because as you continue to fuck your way through your twenties and thirties (and if you're a cougar, your forties and fifties), the list of people you have to call and inform of your "situation" will only get longer and longer. And who wants to have to get back in touch with that douchey guy from your old job you hooked up with in the mailroom after your work birthday party where you were high on a foolish combo of buttercream frosting, Botox, and boxed wine?

Since some STDs are undetectable, a condom, while certainly your first defense, won't even totally protect you. Unless you completely abstain, you can't guarantee you won't get an STD. And if you're reading this book, I assume you're not exactly the president of the abstinence club. So every time you have sex, you're taking a chance that you might end up with a prescription for Valtrex. And you know I love to gamble. But only when the odds are in my favor.

That wasn't exactly the case for my poor friend G. She was absolutely cocksessed* with some cock she'd never even had. She was determined to get this guy despite noticing that Mr. VD* had a series of cold sores that followed a series of hooker-ish girlfriends. Love may be blind, but lust sees all your warts and faults and needs to rub its vagina on you anyway.

After stalking him for a full year, one night she finally found her opening and didn't hesitate to pounce. Girlfriend was straight up in love, she said. He was "the one." She didn't care that she occasionally had a pus-filled sore front-and-center on her mouth every now and then. Luckily, G worked at home. And what's a little STD in the face of eternity?

Cut to two months later when G caught him in the act of passing along his herpes to a stripper at Cheetah's (and not to the lips on her face). She's no longer with Mr. VD, but she has a lifetime reminder of his love every time she gets stressed out.

DEPRAVED fact

One in five Americans have an STD. Five in five men who have dated Paris Hilton have an STD.

BE A
SUPER TEASE

I'm not saying you need to play hard to get to get a guy. But once you know you have him, it is fun to make him cream at the thought of what you'll do to him when he gets to have you.

Whereas a standard tease would make him want you, then hold out having sex with him until he's about to die of blue balls, a super tease lets him know that you ARE going to fuck him imminently, you're just going to make sure he really wants it before you do.

I once pulled the super tease on a coworker at a client dinner while our boss was just inches away. Our office had a strict no-dating policy and he was uber-ambitious, which is the only reason we hadn't fucked yet. But after a few glasses of cabernet before dinner, washed down with a couple of Ritalin, I was determined to change that.

I knew it wouldn't be easy. He was as rigid about the rules as I hoped his cock would be later. Which is why I had to take things to another level. I couldn't just order a sex on the beach or eat my spaghetti suggestively; this was some real varsity shit I'd have to pull.

While we were led to our table, I made sure I was right next to him and then "accidentally" spilled the contents of my ho-kit right in front of him. It was no big deal when the condoms came out, but as he was helping me put my Anal Eaze, pocket rocket, and handcuffs back into my bag, his eyes widened just a bit. I knew it was on.

After our entrées were cleared, he excused himself to go to the bathroom. I followed about two minutes later and stood outside the men's room, waiting for him to come back out. As soon as he appeared, I gave him my panties, telling him I wanted them back in the morning. For the first time since we started working together, he was literally at a loss for words.

The check came, and while our boss was settling the bill, I snuck my cell phone underneath the table and snapped a pic of my bare beaver. I then texted it to him across the table with the message "meet me in the alley behind the restaurant after dinner" and watched as he struggled against the boner that was obviously forming beneath his napkin.

I had a shit-eating grin on my face as we said goodbye to our boss. He thought it was because I felt the dinner was a huge success, but I could really give a fuck about work; I was more concerned with the fuck I was about to get later.

Ten minutes later, we were tangled up in the alley, his mouth on my neck and my hand on his cock as he struggled to get his pants down. But my super tease (combined with my kung fu grip) was just too strong, because by the time we got to the end of the block, he had jizzed in his pants. Embarrassed, he walked me to my car and we never spoke again, except when we had to at work. I guess there may be some cases where just the standard tease is enough!

STANDARD TEASE VS. SUPER TEASE

Standard Tease	Super Tease
Give him a glimpse of a bra strap.	Nip slip.
Work sex into the conversation.	Show him your sex tape on YouTube.
Subtly imply he might get lucky.	Start the fuck countdown timer.

ARE YOU A THRILL FUCKER*?

You may think you are one adventurous bitch in (and out of) bed, but can you look in the mirror and seriously call yourself a thrill fucker? This quiz will help determine if you deserve the coveted title.

1. After you spend the afternoon day-drinking at your favorite dive bar, you decide to spend the night with the guy who bought you all those top-shelf drinks. When you arrive at his apartment, you discover his roommate is home watching television. You:

    a) go straight to Captain Morgan's room, lock the door, turn out the lights, and stuff a towel under the door.

    b) invite the roommate to join.

    c) keep the door open and have sex as loud as you want to.

2. Which car is the most comfortable to have sex in?

   a) Toyota Prius

   b) 1969 Chevy Camaro

   c) Fuck that, I like motorcycles.

3. You meet your latest lust at your favorite little Italian restaurant. Soon after the first bread stick is served, you decide you want to jump his dick. Where do you go?

   a) You give him a BJ under the table before taking him out to the alley and fucking him next to the dumpsters.

   b) Closest apartment. His or yours, it doesn't matter.

   c) Restaurant bathroom. The faux marble counters are a delight.

4. It's your birthday. Your man surprises you with a trip to a theme park. Which attraction is the best for sex?

   a) On a rollercoaster.

   b) In a haunted house.

   c) With the theme park mascot. You've always wanted to try a furry.

5. While on vacation, you spend the day combing the beach-front for seashells and easy sex. You meet a local surfer who suggests you head down to the beach for a quickie. How do you feel about storming the beaches?

a) The thought of having sex on the sand makes my lady bits pucker.

b) I might consider having sex on the beach if it is empty and there are blankets.

c) Sex on the beach? Didn't that bartender invent the drink after he met me?

6. When deciding on a Friday night spot, what criterion do you use to choose a restaurant?

a) The popularity.

b) The price.

c) The availability of bathrooms to have sex in.

7. When your guy asks if he can bring a third into the bedroom, you:

a) ask one of your girlfriends to join you.

b) show up at his house with a hot bi guy ready to have a devil's threesome.*

c) tell him you're not really into ménage à trois.

8. It's 10:30 a.m. and you're at work fucking around online when you suddenly catch yourself nodding off into a sexy daydream. The daydream is about:

a) the last time you had sex with your boyfriend.

b) the last time you had sex with your coworker, Stefan.

c) the last time you had sex with Stefan and your boyfriend watched.

9. Think back to the best experience you've ever had with an airline. What made the trip exceptional?

a) Passed out after washing a fistful of Xanax down with tiny airplane booze bottles stolen from the drink cart.

b) Got bumped up to first class.

c) The pilot taxied down your landing strip.

10. Your fuck buddy decides he wants to be the next Martin Scorsese. He pulls out a camera and asks if you want to have sex with him on film. What do you do?

a) Never in a million years.

b) Agree to do it as long as he promises never to show anyone.

c) Post the finished product on your Facebook page and tag all his friends.

Scoring:

1. a) 1 point; b) 3 points; c) 2 points
2. a) 1 point; b) 2 points; c) 3 points
3. a) 3 points; b) 1 point; c) 2 points
4. a) 2 points; b) 1 point; c) 3 points
5. a) 1 point; b) 2 points; c) 3 points
6. a) 2 points; b) 1 point; c) 3 points
7. a) 2 points; b) 3 points; c) 1 point
8. a) 1 point; b) 2 points; c) 3 points
9. a) 2 points; b) 1 point; c) 3 points
10. a) 1 point; b) 2 points; c) 3 points

Results:

1–10

Congratulations! You must have just graduated from middle school. Either that, or you're one of the dullest fucks around. To you, PDA stands for Public Display of Affection, not Public Displays of Ass. You probably only have sex with a dude after a third date . . . in a bed . . . with the lights off. It's a good thing you picked up this book because it sounds like your sex life is in need of some fucking excitement. Go back to the beginning and re-take this quiz after you've been able to follow at least half of these rules.

11–20

You like to do it in unusual places but you don't like to get caught. You walk the line between adventurous sorority girl and Depraved Girl with ease. One of these days you may have too many sake bombs and fall off into the dark side, but until then, you're happy to be in a polyamorous relationship with your dude, your vibe, and your imagination. Keep reading.

21–30

You are most definitely a thrill fucker. You'll have sex anywhere, anytime, and you get off on not just the possibility of getting caught, but also actually getting caught. In fact, you're so adventurous, you may be reading this while in the hospital—or jail. You could probably add a few of your own depraved rules to this book. Fuck on, my depraved friend. Fuck on.

NEVER FALL FOR YOUR FOR YOUR FUCK BUDDY

I've said it before and I'll say it again: a good steady fuck can be harder to find than a pair of dry panties at a Jonas Brothers concert, so why ruin a good thing by trying to get all romantical on the guy?

If you're lucky enough to have a fuck buddy, do yourself a favor and just be happy you have a regular booty call. Don't wreck it because you have this stupid idea that love (or at least like) and sex have to go together. They don't. In fact, some of the best sex you'll ever have is with a guy you either hate or just met. (Or you don't know him long enough to hate him—yet.)

So many women have a hard time separating sex from romance that suddenly the guy they previously had said only about six words to (those words being "harder," faster," and "that's the wrong hole") becomes someone they fantasize about dying of old age with—or liver disease, whichever comes first—just because he's had his dick in her vagina/ass/mouth. Cuntinis, just because sex gives you that warm fuzzy feeling (also known as an orgasm) it does not equal love.

My friend T made this very mistake not too long ago when she started to develop "feelings" for her fuck and decided to invite him out on a date. There was dinner, there were drinks, but at the end of the night, there was no dick. She said it would have felt "weird" to have sex with him at the end of what was officially their first date. Now, this was a guy whose tongue had been so far inside her vagina that she once said it felt like he was licking her ovary, but suddenly she was shy?

This went on for another date or so, but then her vagina got the best of her and after dinner, she asked him to come inside. To her surprise, he declined, giving her a kiss on the cheek at her doorstep instead. At first, she thought he was being sweet and gentlemanly, but after date no. 5, she was horny and concerned.

"Why don't you want to have sex?" she blurted out one night after four mojitos.

"Well, I'm dating you now," he said.

"Yeah, and?"

"Well, when I was fucking you, I was seeing someone else. Now that we're dating, I'm fucking someone else," he explained. No joke.

T flipped the fuck out. They were so sexually compatible that once her feelings started creeping in, it was impossible for her not to concoct this whole fantasy relationship around him. Which, to her, included monogamy. Funny thing is, he *was* being monogamous. Just not with her.

So after our pity party when she barfed up two Vicodins, three vodka tonics, and a Pinkberry, I asked her if getting dumped by a douche was worth losing some amazing sex.

Her answer? "I'd rather get fucked than fucked over." And that, cunts and queefs, is why you should never fall for your fuck buddy.

HOW TO TURN A FRIEND INTO A FUCK BUDDY

A Depraved Girl should always have a booty call or two in reserve, but if you find yourself tapped out of tappable ass, here's how you can turn a friend into a fuck buddy with my simple, three-pronged approach.

First: isolate your target.

Second: get him drunk.

Third: pounce like a cougar on college night.

If that doesn't work, there's always the roofie colada.

IF HE ASKS YOU TO GO DUTCH, DON'T EVEN THINK ABOUT SHOWING HIM YOUR BRAZILIAN

Let me start off by saying that I am not the kind of girl who thinks that the guy should always pay, no matter what. But "going Dutch" is for pussies who will never see mine if they try to make me split the bill.

I've got no problem paying my own way—in fact, I'll even pay his way too when it's my turn—but way to suck any sexual tension right out of the room if you have to stop and get out your calculator and figure out who owes what.

Once, I somehow got the hottest guy I've ever masturbated over to ask me out to dinner. Halfway through the appetizer, I had to go get a paper towel to put down on my chair, I was that wet for him. To say I was eye-fucking him from across the table would be an understatement.

By the time our entrées came, I was giving him a serious foot job, which was kind of embarrassing for him when the server tried to rearrange the napkin on his lap. I couldn't wait to get the check, get him home, and tear his clothes off. The waiter brought the bill and instead of saying, "Let's get outta here and go fuck," he said, "Wanna go Dutch?" My vag dried up faster than the Sahara.

After he was finished figuring out who owed what and the bill was split, I decided to split myself and left him in the restaurant waiting for me to come back from the bathroom. Oh, and I had driven us there, so the cheap asshole didn't have anyone to split the cab he had to call to get home from the place.

Not wanting to waste my best dress-to-get-laid outfit, I headed to my neighborhood dive bar and sat myself down right next to a "homeless hot" guy. You know, a cute guy who didn't look like he could even afford the free token you needed to get into the bathroom. But when he offered to buy me a PBR,* knowing it was all he could afford, I suddenly found my seat wet again.

I took him home with me and after a good scrub in the shower, we had amazing sex. Oh, and he did ask me to split something that night, but it was my legs so he could give me some surprisingly inventive cunnilingus.

A dinner with a guy should be nothing more than a form of oral foreplay. If he's thinking about money at the end of a meal instead of making a meal out of you, then he's not a guy who's gonna take you home and fuck you good.

DEPRA∨ED fact

Did you know "Dutch" originated from the word "douche"?

If he asks you to split a check, here's other things he may want to split:

- His time between you and his friends.
- His time between you and his girlfriend.
- Your fuck time, and go down on each other instead.
- The sex, according to what it takes to get off. If he says, "My meal was only $17.00, so that's how much I'll contribute to the check," in bed he may say, "I only need forty-five seconds to get off so that's how much I'm willing to contribute."

Say it with me: hell fucking no.

AS LONG AS HE'S STRAIGHT, IT DOESN'T MATTER WHETHER OR NOT HIS TEETH ARE

Us girls are some picky bitches. I have seen many a woman pass up some perfectly good peen because the guy never had braces or is too short or a baldie.

Unless you're British, bad teeth can be a big turnoff for chicks (especially if you have the kind of crooked chompers that easily get food stuck in them, blech!). But bad teeth don't get in the way of good cunnilingus, so who the fuck cares? If his third-world smile bums you out that much, tell him you get turned on by "mute sex" and force him to shut his mouth in bed.

Besides, I know many a guy with perfect teeth who still have to sleep with retainers in order to keep them looking perfect. Have you ever snagged one of those things on a pube? It's not fun.

My friend E is less than five feet tall, but refuses to get with anyone under five-foot-six. She actually carries around a tape measure that says "you must be at least this tall to ride this ride." She once turned down a famous musician (before he was famous) because he was a quarter inch under her height requirement. He later took pics of his enormous peen—which on him, literally looked like a third leg—and posted them on the Internet, but by then, she had missed the fuck out. Now I can kind of understand if you're five-foot-eleven and he's just under Tom Cruise height, that could be kind of awkward, but as long as your genitals line up, who cares if you're staring at the top of his head during sex?

I'm a pretty compact slut at only five-foot-three, and I once dated a guy who was six-foot-four. When we walked down the street together, we could never have a conversation without needing a trip to the chiropractor afterward. But who needs to talk during a relationship? My face was pretty much even with his waist, which meant BJs were so much easier; no knee pads required!

Another friend, J, actively seeks out the baldies because they are so often overlooked, they're like an untapped resource. Plus, she swears that bald dudes are ferosh in the sack. But not ALL bald dudes of course. There are three types of baldies: the stereotypical comb-over dude, who looks like your pedo uncle; the rich bald guy who will pay your rent and fly you and your girlfriends to Vegas for the weekend; and the athletic MMA/ju jitsu/krav maga bald guy who was super-gorge when he had hair (which is the type J goes for).

Unless you're into that sort of thing, I'd stay away from the comb-over guy if you don't want to get stuck in an underground rape bunker or an Olive Garden dinner rush.

The rich guy is obviously good for all the shit you can't afford, and if you've never taken advantage of that kind of relationship, I would at least do it once in your life (every girl deserves a Chanel bag!). But sex with this type of baldie generally tends to be all about him, since if he's paying your way, he feels like he deserves a little diddling in return.

Now, the best type of baldie is obviously the athletic type. Not only can you put a hat on him and he's hot all over again (tell him you have a hat fetish if you want to keep this effect while you're banging), but this dude is usually super aggressive in and out of bed. And he also has his advantages, like intimidating a douchey ex or playing out that prison guard fantasy.

So before you pass up the fat guy, the uncircumcised guy, or the Republican, remember that it's not the little things that matter, it's the big dicks you could be missing out on because you're sweating the small stuff.

IF YOU'RE GONNA GONNA BE A BITCH, BE A MEGA BITCH

You've heard it a million times before: go big or go home. Well, the same rule that applies to bong hits, high school football, and orgies also applies to bitchery.

I'm not saying you should go out there and be cunty to everyone who crosses your peep-toe booties, but if you are going to be a bitch, might as well be queen bitch. You can use this rule when dealing with guys, your coworkers, and most of all, other bitches.

One night I went to see a friend's band play at the Hotel Café with one of my girlfriends. We were standing at the bar with our vodka tonics in hand when a curvy girl squeezed in next to us. She was rocking this Pucci-esque minidress that we were admiring, so my friend asked her where she got it.

"I'm not telling you," she said.

"Why not?"

She looked my friend up and down before she said, "Because it wouldn't look good on you." Bitch!

We were too shocked to respond then and there with a bitch slap before she got her drink and went to sit down at a table, but I wasn't gonna let her get away with that. I was going to be the bigger bitch.

I asked the bartender if I could borrow a pair of scissors; then I walked over to the curvy girl (who was sitting with her back to me), grabbed her dress tag, and snipped. I triumphantly held the tag over my head as my girl clapped for me. You should have seen that bitch's face. She looked mortified.

That's when I read the label: LANE BRYANT. For those of you skinny bitches who shop for tees at Baby Gap, that's the big girls' store. I walked back over to my friend, who was clapping for me at the bar.

"So? Where was the dress from?" my girlfriend asked.

"Well, I may be a mega bitch, but she's definitely the bigger bitch," I said as I showed her the tag. "Bigger as in plus-sized."

My friend almost spit out her vodka tonic. "Ew, Lane Bryant?

No wonder she didn't want to tell me where she got it. She didn't want us to know she was rocking a size sixteen frock," she laughed.

As I looked over at the big bitch, I kind of started to feel something tingling way down in my cold black heart. Was it sympathy?

"What, you want to go apologize?" my friend asked.

"Fuck no," I said, reminding her of Rule #4. But I felt I should do *something*. So I asked the bartender to send her over a drink: rum and *Diet* Coke.

NEVER TRUST A GUY WHO PREFERS BJs TO BANGING

Because he's either

(a) a selfish prick or

(b) gay.

ALWAYS GO
FOR DICKS
OVER PUSSIES
(UNLESS THAT
DICK IS LIMP)

There are pretty much just two types of guys in the world: dicks and pussies.

Dicks are those dirty hot guys who never call after fucking you, text another girl while they're out with you, and after you haven't heard from them for two whole months, ask to borrow $500 (which you happily oblige, only for the chance to have a déjà fuck*).

A pussy calls you every night at the same time, asks your permission before kissing you, and refuses to let you pay for dinner. Sounds dreamy, right?

Wrong.

Sure, a pussy is good for a free meal and an ego boost every now and then, but do you actually want to hook up with a guy whose personality reminds you of your vagenitals*? We bitches aren't getting any younger. Why waste your time with the male equivalent of France, when you could be out there having amazing slutventures with a dirty hot dick?

My friend P was once dating two guys at once: a dick, who for some reason was making it very difficult for her to get into his pants (which of course only made her want to even more), and a pussy who practically got down on his knees at the end of every date.

I asked her why she didn't just ditch the puss and concentrate her total energy on getting that dick. She said she was halfway through a five-star restaurant tour of Chicago and didn't want to dump the guy before she got to eat at Alinea.

After several more dates with each, she found herself getting increasingly horny while continuing to be denied by the dick, and getting fatter after every five-star dinner with the pussy. She knew time was running out to close the deal with the dick, whose interest was beginning to wane. She needed to pounce before she gained so much weight eating the finest Chicago cuisine that she no longer fit into her sexiest skinny jeans. The ones where you could practically see the outline of her vagina.

The night the pussy had made a reservation for the two of them at Alinea, she got a text from the dick asking if she wanted to join him for drinks at a dive bar near his house. She promptly called the pussy with some lame-ass excuse and told the dick she'd meet him there at 8:30. At eight p.m., she showed up at his house instead of the bar and attacked him as soon as he

DEPRA∨ED fact

Seventy-five percent of engaged men are pussies. Seventy-five percent of married men are dicks.

answered the door. She kissed him hard and fast, backing him up to his bedroom.

Before he could stop her, she had his pants down around his ankles. The dick's dick was limp, so she dropped to her knees and started giving him a BJ. After about ten minutes of this (and she prided herself on her excellent BJ skills), there was still no wood. He gave her some sort of excuse about just having jacked off but by the look in his eyes, she knew he was lying. No wonder he was such a dick. You would be too if you were walking around with a limp one.

She called the pussy and asked if it was too late to make their reservation. He said it wasn't, and after eating out at one of the best restaurants in the country, she took him home and let him eat her out.

THERE'S ALWAYS A BACK DOOR

Anal is a great alternative to the vagina when you have a three-day bangover, but this rule is not solely about butt sex. Us Depraved Girls are always stirring up drama, so it's good to know—in any situation—where the back door is.

My girlfriend A was after this dirty hot older guy for years, but whenever she was single, he had a girlfriend and vice versa. Their relationship statuses finally aligned, and when she ran into him at the Echo, he proceeded to engage in some hard-core flirting and she knew it was on.

He invited her back to his house before the last band even went on. A had been indulging in a little nose candy that evening (of the coke variety) and her stomach was already gurgling, but she couldn't pass up the opportunity to get with the guy who was rumored to have a magic tongue.

When they got to his house, she immediately had to run to the bathroom. It was a windowless room, she told me, with no matches, air freshener, or Glade plug-in in sight, but she was already prairie-dogging* and had no choice. Needless to say, she took the biggest, stankiest coke dump in the history of womankind. It was so horrible that the smell in that small room almost made her add some puke to the already overflowing toilet bowl.

The stink was already beginning to waft down the hallway, so what did A do? She made sure the coast was clear before she hoofed it out the back door and never spoke to him again.

So when the Chyna look-alike you threatened to punch in vagina last week walks into the bar, when the guy you ditched ook up with your latest lust turns up at the same party, or

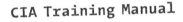

CIA Training Manual

When entering a building:

1. Analyze architecture and find all exits.

2. Discern air flow patterns for potential chemical attacks.

3. Determine acoustics of various rooms to avoid revealing discreet information.

4. Never enter a vulnerable situation without proper gear and equipment.

when your boss takes her lunch at Barney's on the day you called in sick to shop the sales, remember, there is ALWAYS a back door.

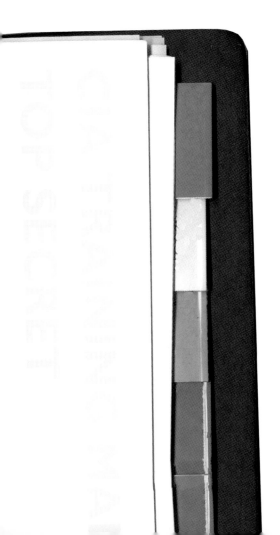

HOW TO STEALTH POO
AT YOUR HOOKUP'S HOUSE

After a night spent drinking, smoking, and dancing (along with a late-night drunken binge on chili cheese fries), every girl may be tempted to make a bowel movement—or two. But what do you do when you get the uncontrollable urge to poo at your hookup's house and there aren't any matchbooks in sight? Fear not, my depraved sistas. Luckily I've done the dirty work for you so you'll never have to make an excuse to run down to his apartment lobby again.

I can pretty much drop a deuce anywhere—work, gas stations, behind the DJ tent at Coachella (bad example)—but I couldn't poo at the house of a cute guy I was about to have sex with until I discovered these must-read tips:

• Turn on the water while you're dumping. There's nothing worse than an escaping wet fart to let your dude know you're doing the doo. You must make sure you wash your hands after, or he'll get suspicious if they still smell like the ciggy you shared on the way home.

• My girlfriend swears by the courtesy flush. As soon as your log hits the water, flush the toilet and it supposedly dissipates the smell.

• Open a window, but whatever you do, DO NOT TURN ON THE FAN. That's a sure sign you're shitting.

• If you're truly a Depraved Girl, you're always prepared (Rule #12) and will keep a bottle of Poo-Pourri stocked in your slag-bag. What's Poo-Pourri? An ingenious little air-freshener you spray in the bowl before you go. It eliminates the smell of your toxic dump as it gets flushed down the toilet.

• If you absolutely have no tools at your disposal to dispel your dump smell, just shut the door and immediately attack him in whatever room is farthest from the bathroom. Make sure you extend the foreplay for as long as you can. If he's a three-minute man, chances are he'll be running for the bathroom the minute he's shot his load—and then you'll be busted.

RELATIONSHIPS ARE GREAT WHEN YOU DON'T GIVE A SHIT

I was never really the relationship type. I'd usually date a guy long enough to know the shape of the mole on his scrotum—and then we'd break up. Why? Because relationships suck—unless you don't give a shit.

Think about it. Sex is the entire reason you started seeing this guy. The sex was hot, it was spontaneous, it took place in strange locations, and you could never get enough. Once you two agreed you would only fuck each other and no one else, the sex started to take place after dinner instead of drinks, and mostly in your bed. Then when you started calling each other "girlfriend" and "boyfriend" and moved in together, the sex started to decline.

Maybe because it was just there all the time and neither one of you had to work for it, but you went from fucking every single night (and more than once) to just a few times a week. He was working late, you were busy organizing a pity party for your friend who just got dumped, and at the end of the day, you were too tired and/or fucked up on vikes* to find each other's genitals.

Then you start getting paranoid. Sure, you've been hitting Pinkberry a lot lately, but is he not fucking you because you gained four pounds? And when he leaves his skidmark-stained manties* all over the bathroom, does that mean he no longer loves you?

Pretty soon, he's finding excuses not to come home and you're finding excuses to stay home crying into your bottle of vodka while you wait up for him, certain he's fucking a stripper from Cheetah's.

He finally comes home at three a.m., and in your fucked-up state, you manage to start a fight ten times louder than the ones between the trannies on Santa Monica Boulevard. While trying to throw whatever objects you can grasp at him, you stumble and he reaches out to catch you, but you immediately jump back, certain he's about to hit you. You call the cops (who were already on their way because the neighbors are tired of this shit) and claim he hit you, and he has to spend the night in the station giving his statement.

Even though you recant and apologize and tell him to come home, he spends the night at a friend's house, which you're sure is the house of the stripper from Cheetah's, and you call him fifty times to scream unintelligible obscenities at him on his voicemail which he never picks up.

In the morning, you cry and call him fifty times to beg him to come home. Then your parents get involved and forbid you to see the woman-beater; you get all teenage-y on them and say "but I love him, Dad!" and only want to get back with him even more. But by then he's had enough of your bowlful of crazy and has moved out. You're so devastated that you spend a month in bed with nothing but a bottle of vodka and an endless supply of Xanax and sleeping pills, convinced he was the perfect man for you and you'll never love again.

Sound familiar?

One of the most successful long-term relationships I ever witnessed was between my friend B and this guy she couldn't give two fucks about. It was a particularly apathetic period of her life, and after being pursued relentlessly by this guy she'd fuck on occasion because he had the most awesome concert ticket hookup, she finally decided to give in.

He paid her rent, took her to the best restaurants, went down on her every night, and they never fought. She could stay out all night partying with her girlfriends, never returning his calls, and he never said a bad word to her. This went on for the better part of two years.

Then one particularly wild and drunken girls' night out turned into a particularly wild and drunken girls' weekend out. He started blowing up her phone, which she simply switched off. When she finally came to early Monday morning, she listened to her messages. He had gotten into a semiserious car accident and needed her to pick him up from the hospital. When she never showed up, he finally decided he'd had enough of her bullshit and texted her two words: "We're through." She simply shrugged and deleted his number from her phone.

To this day, she still says it was the best relationship she ever had.

DOUCHES ARE BAD FOR YOUR VAGINA

It's not hard for the inexperienced bitch to get sucked in by a cocky asshole with a fake tan and bleached teeth, but I'm here to tell you girls that douches are bad for your vagina.

I'm the first one to tell you to fuck first and ask questions later (as long as you're safe), but hooking up with those hard-to-resist D-bags has its consequences.

I knew the sweetest girl, N, who was practically a virgin when she moved to LA. Her first month here, she decided to put on the hottest dress she could afford from Forever 21 and go solo to whatever Hollywood club was popular at the time, hoping to rub tits with some famous people. She said she was there for a full hour before anyone even talked to her (even the bartender).

Finally, she was approached by a guy who was one of those buttergears. You know, hot except for his horrible taste in clothes? He was wearing a button-down shirt with a flower em-broidered on the front, which is like chick repellent to most Depraved Girls. But she was fresh off the bus and hypnotized by the two-carat diamond studs in each of his ears. Plus, he was dropping names of all the celebs he could introduce her to, and even though she was wasted off of her first glass of chardonnay, he continued buying her drinks all night so she couldn't resist.

Even though she would never have sex with someone she just met back at home, N told me she wanted to embrace a new, more adventurous identity here in Hollywood, so she accepted his invitation to go home and check out his condom collection—a line so douchey it would barely even fly at the Jersey Shore. But she was drunk, she was grateful for the attention, and she was ready to break her LA cherry.

Well, her cherry almost broke after two minutes in bed with him—they had frat boy sex. You know, where the guy pretty much is just jacking off inside you? Of course, he had no lube either, so her vag was rubbed raw. She later told me she felt like she had a rope burn inside her puss; she was surprised no smoke came out while he was humping her like a rabbit. Poor thing had a bangover that lasted a week. Of course, it was several months before she'd ever attempt to fuck a guy in Hollywood again, and this time, she was certain to bring lube with her.

But you can't fault N for going home with a douche. We've all been susceptible to douchebaggery when we're desperate, horny, and looking at guys through beer goggles thicker than the glass on the popemobile. There's no shame in getting yours, but if you suspect you may have hooked up with a douchebag, you may want to *Coyote Ugly* yourself stat.

HOW TO TELL IF YOU'VE JUST HOOKED UP WITH A DOUCHEBAG

that doesn't necessarily mean he's even bi, because sometimes it's just about the sex, not the sexuality.

Many a fruit fly has lost her main gay by not realizing that a horny gay man will sometimes fuck anything when he's had enough strawberry mojitos—even her. Don't mistake his dick falling into the nearest open orifice (in this case, your vag) for the idea that he could go straight for you, and that the two of you would live glittery ever after.

Because there's nothing more ruthless than a gay who perceives a future cock-blocker. He'll cut you out of his iPhone faster than you can say "Fred Segal." Of all the unavailable men Depraved Girls obsess over, do yourself a favor and forget this one. Fucking forget it right now.

DEPRAⱯED fact

Fifty-four percent of gay guys polled said they would fuck a female friend if they are horny enough, drunk enough, and their Grindr iPhone app is malfunctioning.

HOW TO TELL IF
HE'S GAY OR JUST BRITISH

You know how sometimes you spot a hot guy, but he's sporting about ten ounces of man-gel, a gank top (gay tank top), or a button-down so you immediately assume he's gay? Well, sometimes he's not gay, he's just British—and you walked away from some perfectly willing dick!

You really can't be sure until you get close enough to hear an accent, but if you don't want to make the walk across the room only to find out he likes butt sex more than you do, here's a few clues you can spot from a distance:

• Teeth. (Duh!) My gays like a bright, straight smile.

• Shoes. British guys like gayer footwear than the gays. If he's wearing Converse, chances are he's playing for the other team.

• Beer bellies. The Brits tend to be a bit soft. If he's got one, he could be straight.

DEVELOP A MAGIC PUSSY

You're sitting at the bar and you're talking to this guy. He's hot, he's funny, he's smart, and there's a very good possibility he's straight. He says something mildly amusing, you throw your head back and laugh, putting your hand over his for emphasis. That's when you see it: he's wearing a wedding ring.

Come to think of it, he's not even flirting with you, he's just being charmingly polite. But before you can turn your head, a woman's hand snakes around his neck. First you notice the two-carat diamond. Then you notice the fabulous Lanvin top. Then you notice the face and you almost do a spit take right into Mr. Perfect's face.

Bitch is beat.

Your first thought: sugar mama. But HE picks up the tab. So how did someone as ugly as her get someone as amazing as him? Easy. She has a magic pussy.

What's a magic pussy, you ask? I'm sure visions of a Thai ping-pong show are running through your head, but that's not magic, just a lot of control. A magic pussy is when a woman un-worthy of a fantastic man has him so P-whipped that he won't even take a shit without her say-so. Examples of famous magic pussies past and present: Wallis Simpson, the fugly, premeno-pausal, thrice-divorced American woman who made a British king abdicate his throne. And Kate Hudson. Even with eyes set as far apart as a hammerhead shark's, she's got musicians, actors, and athletes alike slitting their wrists at the thought of losing her.

So how do you get one?

Well, forget about doing your Kegels. It's all about confidence. The ugliest woman can have a guy wrapped around her little finger if she makes him think he's lucky to have her. I once knew a girl who would whisper things in her guy's ear when he was asleep like, "You're so lucky to have me . . . you'd die if I ever left you . . . you'd jump off a bridge if I broke up with you," and crazy shit like that.

I knew another girl who had a crush on a coworker, so when he was at lunch, she'd stick her finger up her crotch and rub her 'gina juice all over his keyboard until one day he just knew he had to have her.

So practice one of these techniques or try out your own, but remember, once your vag is magic, you can get any guy you want.

MAGIC PUSSY

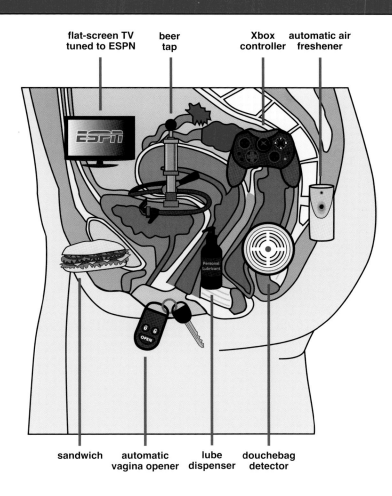

flat-screen TV tuned to ESPN

beer tap

Xbox controller

automatic air freshener

sandwich

automatic vagina opener

lube dispenser

douchebag detector

NEVER FALL IN LOVE WITH A GUY YOU MEET IN A BAR

I know all you depraved bitches are going, "Where the fuck else am I gonna meet a guy?" but guys in bars are only good for two things: free drinks and meaningless sex.

Now I'm not saying that should stop you from picking up dudes in bars; on the contrary, it's a great place to meet a good fuck, but whatever you do, do not make the mistake of actually establishing a relationship with the fucker. It will go bad faster than a celebrity marriage. Of course, it's hard to know when you meet a guy at a bar exactly what category he may fall into—friend with benefits, fuck buddy, stalkee, ex-boyfriend—but do yourself a favor and cut shit off before it gets anywhere near the dreaded "relationship" stage.

Back when I was a very young and naive slut, I met a guy one night at my regular watering hole. This was so long ago that people still smoked in bars, so after I used my favorite pickup line— "Gotta light?"—we were pretty much inseparable for months.

This guy was like the Holy Grail of dudes: he gave me the most incredible head without even wanting reciprocation. (Yes, Virginia, there is a Pussy Claus.) So after a while of dating Mr. Wonderful, I broke my own rule—I was starting to fall for him.

In fact, it was getting so serious that I thought it was time to have "the talk." He took me out to my favorite restaurant, the one that serves the best liquid appetizers (that's code for alcohol, bitches), so I figured it was the perfect moment. After about five vodka tonics, which I washed down with a side salad, he said he wanted to talk to me about something. OMG, I thought, we're totes on the same page!

"I think we should stop seeing each other," he said.

"Ummm, excuse me?"

"Well, what did you expect?" he said. "We met at a bar."

HOW TO TELL A MAN BY HIS DRINK

Douchebag	Bottle service, vodka Red Bull
Dirty Hot Guy	Whiskey, bourbon, scotch, any liquor served neat
Frat Boy	Whatever beer is cheapest, Jäeger bombs
Dick	Imported beer, old-timey drinks like a Manhattan or a gin fizz
Pussy	He'll have whatever you're having

BREAKUP SEX IS ALMOST ALWAYS BETTER THAN MAKEUP SEX

I love a good fuck at the end of a breakup. It's like a handshake after finalizing business negotiations—it seals the deal.

You're already worked up over who's taking custody of your sex tape, and besides, there's nothing better after hours of screaming, crying, and threatening to cut the cat in two if he won't let you have it than some hot hate sex. Besides, you're both putting on your best performances because you know it's the measuring stick you'll both be comparing your next hookups to. Breakup sex is a final goodbye, a fuck you and a fuck me all in one.

What's not so hot is the overly emotional and romantical makeup sex with the guy you once called "Satan's left nut" when you cave months later. Sure, after weeks of bad dates and worse one-night-stands, it feels good to have sex with someone who knows where to find your clit. But don't confuse "familiar" with "I've given up hope of ever finding someone who not only knows where to find my clit, but actually uses that knowledge on more than a monthly basis."

We've all been tempted, but don't turn your bonus night into makeup sex and decide to settle for this asshole because you're too lazy to put on your slut top and fuck-me stilettos to go look for a new asshole. Because as I said before in Rule #19, settling is for quitters. And Depraved Girls are definitely not quitters.

There's nothing wrong with a déjà fuck, but a déjà relationship never works. You already know all his stories, quirks, bad habits, and where he keeps his coke stash, so the thrill of discovery is gone. Which means your second honeymoon period lasts about as long as the makeup sex.

Don't be pulled in by his promises that everything is going to be different this time, that he'll spend less time trying to get to the next level of Halo and more time trying to get you to your next level of orgasm. (Yeah, there's different levels, didn't you know?) Because people don't really change. And the dick you know is certainly less exciting than the dick you don't. Well, unless that dick turns out to be a limp three inches.

The best part about breakup sex is that as soon as it's over, you no longer want to murder your ex. But as soon as the makeup sex is over, you're ready to stab him again. So do yourself a favor and quit while you're ahead. Because breakup sex is all about "me." And makeup sex is all about "us." And you've already decided you don't want an "us."

But what if the sex is so mind-blowingly fantastic, even though you want to break up with him, you just can't bring yourself to cut it off?

I had that problem with the last truly assholian guy I dated. A beautifully damaged, manipulative bipolar alcoholic drug addict, this guy had it all. But he was also obsessively in love with me, which is why it was so hard to break it off. Coke was his drug, but he was mine. Whenever I'd broach the topic of "taking a break" which is just code for a breakup, he'd cry and sob and threaten to go on another NyQuil bender. I also suspected he was cheating on me, but I didn't have proof, which I knew I needed in order to get me to leave.

Desperate, I finally convinced my hot friend L to seduce him and let me catch them right before they started to do the do, where I'd promptly break up with him, and L wouldn't have to add to her already impressive number.

So I showed up at her apartment at our appointed time and threw open the door, ready to shout an "AHA!" (or maybe even a "Caught you, motherfucker!"—I practiced them both). But when I opened the door, I completely forgot my line, because I accidentally witnessed my soon-to-be ex putting his peen in my friend's surprisingly hairy ass. I simply shut the door, shook my head, and walked out, never to talk to either of them again.

HOW TO DUMP A DICK

Sometimes you're dating a guy who's such a prick that even you know he's bad for you. That's when a simple "we're through" or "don't ever call me again" isn't sufficient. Here's how you can give him a send-off worthy of his dickishness:

• If you live together, wait until he's out of town and move all his stuff out on the front lawn. But don't just stop there. Hold a yard sale where you sell everything: his vintage club chair; his skid-marked manties; and his limited edition Radiohead concert posters. Take all the money you made and throw him a huge "going away" party, inviting all your friends. When he comes home to the party, you can finally tell everyone where he's going—the hell away from you.

• If you're arty, you can spend some time on a crafts project at home: grab a recent photo of him and create a series of old-timey "Wanted" posters. Print "Wanted: For Having a 3-inch Cock," or something similarly embarrassing, and make enough copies to paper the poles outside of his work, his house, and his favorite bar.

- When he's passed out drunk in your bed with whiskey dick, grab his car keys. Drive it to a location that has special meaning for you (e.g., where he promised he'd take you on your anniversary but decided to go to Vegas with the boys instead). When he finally comes to, present him with a scavenger hunt list of clues that will eventually lead him to his car. Make sure you take him to the apartment where you caught him cheating on you with his best friend's girlfriend, the bar where he showed up so wasted on your birthday that he puked on all your gifts, and the free clinic you visited when you learned he had given you chlamydia. When he finally finds his ride, make sure the paint is covered in gay pride stickers.

HE DOESN'T HAVE TO BE THAT INTO YOU AS LONG AS HE'S INTO HAVING SEX WITH YOU

Listen, ladies (and I use that term loosely), of course we all want a guy who's willing to cut off his left nut and fist it up his best friend's ass just to get a date with us, but that's not always going to be the case. And that's okay.

Besides, not every encounter needs to lead to a relationship. Hell, it doesn't even need to lead to a date. Sometimes you meet a guy who isn't meant to be one of your great loves, but one of your great fucks. So does it really matter if he's that into you? As long as he's into having sex with you, I say go for it.

I had one friend, Y, who for some reason wouldn't even consider dating a guy who wasn't that into her, let alone fucking him. But my other friend C would only hook up with guys who didn't want to date her. I bet one of these bitches sounds familiar to you. Let's take a look at a typical day in their lives:

Friend "C"

All Calendars **Calendar** +

◀ **Tuesday Aug 27 2012** ▶

9:00 AM She texts him asking if he wants to meet up for a drink that night. No answer.

11:30 AM She spends her morning at work lurking his Facebook and Twitter accounts, looking for any clues of where she might be able to find him later.

1:00 PM She texts him again. Still no answer.

3:30 PM She bribes one of his best friends with her Vicodin prescription—that she was saving from when she had her wisdom teeth pulled—to tell her where he'll be that night.

8:00 PM After work, she drops off the pills with his friend, who tells her his whereabouts.

8:30 PM She takes a quick whore's bath, dresses to get laid, and heads to the bar early so she can grab a seat with a view of the entrance.

12:00 AM She's buying him his fifth whiskey soda and he's finally drunk enough to start to consider going home with her.

1:30 AM The sex is so loud and aggressive the neighbors think she is getting beaten up.

3:00 AM The cops who responded to the domestic call leave.

3:24 AM They go back to bed for round four.

Today | List | Day | Month | ↓

So which would you prefer: the lousy lay who's really into you, or the hot sex with a guy who'll give you multiple orgasms, not multiple dates?

KNOW HOW
AND WHEN
TO MAKE
AN EXIT

While most bitches are concerned with how and when to make an entrance, a Depraved Girl knows that it's really how and when you make an exit that counts. Because you never know when you'll have to beat it out the back door.

For the "how," there's obviously two ways to go: you can either sneak out or be as loud as possible.

I had a guy friend who was a cater waiter and always knew of the best parties where you could drink and eat for free. On one such occasion, he invited us to a shindig at a swanky restaurant on the West Side where they were serving only top-shelf liquor. After he snuck us into the kitchen, I ordered my first Ketel One martini and had downed about four crab cakes when I looked around and realized what event we had crashed.

It was a rehearsal dinner. For the wedding of my ex-boyfriend J. The one who had broken my heart and driven me into a life of depravity. I panicked. He looked so happy and she looked so gorge and I had a zit the size of Texas that not even a pound of concealer could conceal.

"I gotta get the fuck out of here," I said to my girl. Just as we were about to sneak back out the way we had come in, the music stopped, a crowd gathered around us, and a spotlight hit the groom's father, who was standing about three feet to my right. I immediately turned around to face the bar and tried to survey all my exits, but unless I wanted him to notice me, I was trapped.

But then I saw a pack of matches next to a pile of napkins on the bar. Everyone was busy watching the speeches so no one noticed that I had lit a match and was watching as the stack went up in flames. "Fire!" my friend yelled, starting a panic. As everyone ran for the exits, we snuck back out through the kitchen in all the commotion. Taking the top-shelf booze with us, of course.

I spent the rest of the night getting so wasted on the free booze that I accidentally peed into one of my Philippe Starck chairs, mistaking it for a toilet. But that didn't stop me from putting on one of my hottest cocktail dresses with my highest heels, getting my zit covered for free by the makeup ladies at the MAC counter, and dragging my girlfriend with me to my ex's wedding reception the next day. (I had overheard the deets of the location at the rehearsal dinner the previous night.)

Since it was an outdoor affair, getting in was no problem. But here's how I got out: I waited out the speeches from the best man and maid of honor at the bar drinking the top-shelf booze. As soon as the parents had all given a toast and the bride and groom were about to take the floor for the first dance, I jumped up onto the stage with the band and grabbed the mic.

"I just wanted to give one more toast to the bride," I slurred. J's eyes widened when he saw it was me. "It takes a brave woman to marry a guy who fucked his sister." Little did I know that he actually had a sister, and everyone turned to stare at her in shock.

"Let's all raise a glass to Mr. and Mrs. Sister-Fucker!" I threw the microphone down and headed for the exit before they could throw me out, but not before grabbing some free top-shelf liquor from the bar on my way out.

Even in my drunken stupor I knew it was time to get the hell out of there, but you may find yourself in some situations when you're not sure whether you should stay or run screaming for the back door. Don't worry, bitch. I gotchu:

- Your ex walks in with his hot new girlfriend and you are making out with an ugly dude. Get out right away. Take the ugly dude with you if you're horny and desperate (see page 81 for how to fuck an ugly guy).

- You're meeting your online hookup in person for the first time and it turns out he has one tiny arm that you never saw on your video chats (he always jacked it with the other one). Wait until he buys you another drink, shoot it, then excuse yourself to go to the bathroom and climb out of the nearest window.

- Your best gay starts macking with a hot go-go boy on the dance floor of the gay club. Stay and watch. When he starts getting a BJ, that's your cue to take his car and drive your-self home, because he's getting stuck good that night.

when I was approximately two minutes and forty-eight seconds into my self-pleasure. I didn't hear the doorbell over the whir of my vibrator and my own moans, so my bitch roommate answered it. It took her approximately forty-eight seconds to survey the sitch and figure out how to use it to her advantage.

She straight up told my date I was jacking it in the room next door, and ended up going out on my date and drinking my free drinks. The asshole even brought him home that night where I heard her fucking the shit out of him all night.

I got her back, though. In the morning, as he was about to leave, I slipped him some Valtrex I got from Planned Parenthood the night before while they were out on my date. "You might need this," I said, before slamming the door in his face.

He obviously never called her again and every time I saw him in the crowded elevator, I'd ask him with a concerned tilt of my head, "Have you had another outbreak or is the Valtrex keeping the herp in check?" He eventually took a new job in another office about the same time I decided to take up residence in another apartment—alone.

DEPRAVED fact

In ancient Rome, "to masturbate" meant "to prepare for a date or special occasion."

FLAKE ON HIM BEFORE HE FLAKES ON YOU

Why sit around with that horrible pit in your stomach wondering if he's going to blow off the plans he made with you tonight when you can just cut that shit off first and feel like the flaker instead of the flakee?

The days of guys making plans on Wednesday for a Saturday date are long over. But you can still get an indication that he's going to flake on you if he doesn't return your texts the day of your supposed plans. There's nothing worse than spending the day waxing every orifice and putting on your best dress-to-get-laid outfit only to get a call five minutes before you're planning on being fashionably late to hear whatever lame excuse for not coming he's decided to pull out of his ass that night.

Although you should consider yourself lucky if he even gives you an excuse; a lot of guys either text a simple "sorry, babe, have to reschedule" or don't even bother to show at all. If he goes to the trouble to lie to you, he might kind of like you enough to fuck you when he's drunk some time.

The day of what was supposed to be my first date with my now ex-boyfriend, I was so nervous with anticipation for our first fuck that I actually gave myself diarrhea. Nothing that couldn't be corrected with a fistful of Imodium and a few Xannies, but still, it wasn't exactly how I had wanted to spend my Sunday afternoon. My amazing girlfriend M was gracious enough to hang with me for most of the day trying to distract me, but the pit just kept growing with every hour that went by.

I still hadn't heard from him by the early evening, so M called up one of his boys to get some intel on his intentions. Apparently my future ex-boyfriend had been out partying with Tina* all night until two—that's two p.m.—and was about to call me to cancel. "Call him first," she wisely advised me. "That way, you're the one who flaked on him."

I speed-dialed him. Before he could even get a word out, I vomited the best excuse I could think of on the spot. "Yeah, my sister just got kidnapped by a bunch of nuns and my parents are freaking out, so it's kind of a family crisis right now." Who knows if he bought it or if he was relieved I did it to him first, but it worked. Not only did the pit instantly disappear, but I like to think that he was the one who was now freaking out that I was blowing him off.

We made plans again for the next week and after our re-skedded first date, we were inseparable for the next two years. Although in this particular cheating-stripper-fucking case, I might just have been better off if I'd let him blow me off first.

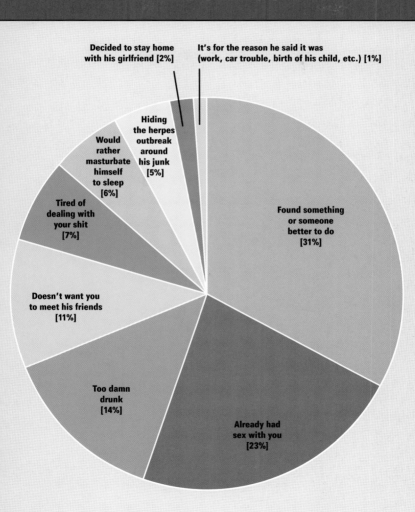

REASONS WHY GUYS FLAKE ON YOU

Decided to stay home with his girlfriend [2%]

It's for the reason he said it was (work, car trouble, birth of his child, etc.) [1%]

Hiding the herpes outbreak around his junk [5%]

Would rather masturbate himself to sleep [6%]

Tired of dealing with your shit [7%]

Doesn't want you to meet his friends [11%]

Too damn drunk [14%]

Already had sex with you [23%]

Found something or someone better to do [31%]

IF YOU'RE TIRED OF PLAYING THE GAME, FIND A GUY WHO DOESN'T KNOW THE RULES

Sometimes you're just tired of all the fuckery that comes along with trying to get fucked. So take a break from the games men play and go find someone who doesn't know the rules: a boy. Now, I'm NOT suggesting pedophilia, but I AM suggesting a little puma-ing!

Whenever I was fed up with chasing men who were running their own little game on me while I was playing with a distinctly different set of rules, I'd go to the one place where I didn't have to put on my game-face—Cabo Cantina.

For those of you who don't live in LA, Cabo Cantina is a post-college mecca for the under-twenty-five crowd. It's like Señor Frog's and Barney's Beanery rolled into one, and on any given night you can scope out some of the hottest boys in town. Emphasis on boys.

On one such evening, me and my thirty-something girlfriends decided to stop at Cabo for a pre-party drink. I quickly spotted one of the hottest guys I've ever seen. He looked like Adrian Grenier, only with an amazing body. He was a model slash personal trainer (of course) and looks-wise way out of my league. But he was only twenty-two and didn't have his game intact yet.

So after the initial "What's your name?" and "What do you do?" I gazed into his gorgeous greens and simply said, "Wanna make out?" He shrugged and said, "Okay!" Since he wasn't yet a player, he had no problem macking on me in the middle of the bar, in full-on view of all the jealous coeds who were throwing me some serious shade for commandeering the hot guy in the room.

We stayed for another drink (which at Cabo is really two drinks) before I suggested moving the party-of-two to his place. Since he had no car (dude drove a bike), I stuffed the two-wheeler in my trunk and headed to the one-bedroom he shared with about four other MAWs (model/actor/whatevers) a few blocks away.

The great thing about fucking young dudes is that they're eager to please. He yanked my pants off so hard they almost ripped, and began enthusiastically, if not expertly, munching on the puss, stopping occasionally to ask me if he was doing it right. Not quite, but close, so eventually we moved on to doing the sex. It was hot, it was enthusiastic, it was over in five minutes. But guess what? In another five minutes he was ready to go again, so we ended up having sex a total of five times and twenty-five minutes in one night.

Sure, I had to stop by the drugstore on my way home to pick up a crab kit, but for a no-brainer of a night, it was worth it!

GUYS WHO
DON'T KNOW THE RULES

Guy Friend	**Pro**	**Con**
College Guys	They're always ready to fuck.	A short and sloppy lay.
Sci-Fi Geeks	You can make them your own personal slave.	You'll have to do it while *Battlestar Galactica* plays in the background.
Hicks Who Just Moved to the City	They're ready to try anything.	They don't know how to DO anything.
Foreigners	They think everything you do is amazing.	They're uncircumcised.

HOW TO
FUCK A VIRGIN

A virgin is like one of America's most precious and rare resources. And like a national park, you should leave it in better condition than when you found it. Finding a male virgin who wouldn't land you in jail for statutory rape is pretty rare, but not impossible (Comic-Con), so here's how you handle the situation should you find yourself in the cherry-popping position:

- **Don't be gentle.** It's the movie preview for the film version of the rest of his life. So make it hot and sweaty, not sweet and romantical.

- **Show rather than tell,** except when it comes to cunnilingus.

- **Be yourself.** Sure, you're the bitch he'll compare all other bitches to in the future, but be yourself, not a better, nicer, more generous version of yourself just because it's his first time. You don't want him to think that all women are that giving. It'll ruin him for the rest of us.

KEEP EVERY DICK PIC A GUY SENDS YOU

Getting a pic of a guy's hard peen via text, IM, or e-mail can be an incredible pick-me-up in the middle of your day. But it can also be a powerful tool should he ever do you wrong.

For instance, take that dirty hot musician you were secretly fucking—his secret, not yours. After you lent him five hundred bucks to buy a new guitar that he said would finally help score him that record deal, but he really went and blew it all on blow and didn't share, and he totally dumped you for a Russian groupie, you can print out that portrait of his three-incher and paper his next "gig" with it, which is really just a friend allowing him to play at a house party.

Before the recent spate of celebrities and politicians who outed themselves by posting dick pics on Twitter, a friend of mine in DC made a pretty good living from all the incentives she received by NOT posting them.

Another friend, P, has catalogued every single naked pic a guy's ever had the indecency to send her. She was once engaging in some serious sexting with an ex who had dumped her for some fashion whore, but now claimed he was recently single. Being the coy bitch that she is, P gave him a look at her breastacles in exchange for a peek at his peen. The minute he texted her the dick pic, she downloaded it to her computer where she saved it and backed that shit up.

Their cell flirting continued for days, but since P couldn't confirm that he was actually broken up with his whore, she never took their sexting off network (P was a bit of a germophobe and refused to get naked with a guy until she could confirm he wasn't fucking anyone else and was STD-free).

P continued looking for some sort of sign that he might be a safe fuck, lurking his Facebook page, and talking to their mutual friends, but when her bestie happened to run into the totally together couple at brunch (the fashion whore had been at a trade show in New York), P knew the asshole had only been sexting her because his girlfriend was out of town.

So she posted his peen pic on her Facebook page and tagged each ball as her ex and his girlfriend. The caption read: "Here's what XXX was doing while his girlfriend was out of town."

DEPRAVED fact

If you regularly gaze at your dick pic collection, you're no longer into revenge; you're now into porn.

IT'S NOT A DATE UNLESS SOMETHING GETS WET

Dating rituals are so confusing these days that my girlfriends are having a terrible time deciphering whether or not the din-ner/coffee/S&M/whatever thing they just went out on would even constitute a date!

The other night my girlfriend E called me after one such "thing." "I went out with this great guy last night," she said.

"Yeah?" I put down my bottle of wine and settled into my couch, getting ready for a great fuck story.

"He picked me up, and even held the car door open for me," she began.

"Uh-huh," I said, hoping she would hurry up and get to the good shit.

"I swear, I haven't laughed so much since the time we hacked into my ex's cell, and he and I weren't even doing anything illegal, we were just having dinner!" She was really starting to kill my buzz with this boring-ass story. "And he even paid for dinner," she said as I was about to kill myself. "So was it a date?" she asked.

I already knew the answer but I went through my checklist anyway. "Did you fuck him?"

"No."

"Blow him?"

"No."

"Get finger banged?"

"No."

"Kiss him, even?"

"He hugged me goodnight when he dropped me off."

"Then guess what, bitch? It's not a date!"

Sometimes we're so desperate for a little male attention that we want to believe that any interaction between a dude and ourselves could constitute the beginning of a romantic relationship, but unless someone's getting fucked, blown, banged, or at least kissed (with tongue), it's nothing more than a free dinner.

I could go out with my best gay and have the time of my life consuming all the fish tacos and double margaritas he can afford at Fiesta Cantina, but since he's not going to be high-fiving my tongue with his penis at the end of the night, it's not a date. (Okay, there was that one time his dick found his way into my mouth after a bottle of absinthe and a couple of Fubar go-go boys, but that's a different story.)

IF you like the guy AND he's taking you to dinner AND he's paying, the least you could do would be to drop to your knees and show him a little appreciation! I guarantee you he won't say no, and at least you'll then be certain of one thing: it was a date!

IS IT A DATE?

AN ORGASM A DAY KEEPS THE DOCTOR AWAY

It cures colds. It keeps you looking young. It's more relaxing (and cheaper!) than a Xantini: an orgasm a day.

Some people may find it a daunting daily task due to a hectic lifestyle, lack of a partner, or bad hand-eye coordination. (Not me. Show me a Jacuzzi jet and I'll show you my jizz.) But ignoring this most basic of instincts can have some serious consequences. You could even end up in the hospital, like me.

After a one-night-stand that started with an orgasm and ended with a herpes scare, I decided to swear off any and all sex, even with myself, for a month. My friends all warned me that I would probably lose my shit and start drowning puppies if I went that long without an O, and since the test had come back negative (turns out it was just an ingrown hair), I should do PETA a favor and at least play with my toys. But I had made a promise to God that I would leave my vagina alone for a month if he spared me from an STD and I was determined to keep it.

But after only one day without my daily shower jerk, I started getting the worst headache. Nothing would cure it, not a trip to the gym, not upping my intake of caffeine, not even a handful of Vicodin.

After about a week, I found it hard to get out of bed and go to work. Not because I couldn't concentrate, but because I found myself wanting to have sex with everyone who crossed my path. It's like I had the worst beer goggles in history; everyone from the trash guy to my boss (who had a mole on his face so big that it looked like a second head) became the target of my sexual fantasy. I eventually had to use up all my sick days to stay home because every time I looked at my boss, I got simultaneously wet and nauseous and I spent more time running to the bathroom than doing my work.

At week four, when I hadn't left my house for days, I got a text from this totally creamy guy I had been trying to hook up with for years. He was moving to London in a few days and wanted to invite me to his going-away party. As luck would have it, he was leaving the day my self-imposed orgasm exile was to end.

I declined the invite to the party. But since his flight wasn't leaving until the next night, I asked if we could get together for brunch instead and he miraculously agreed, saying he'd pick me up the next morning.

The next few days as I waited were excruciating. I did everything I could to try not to think about him, took cold showers, watched Fox News, but when Ann Coulter starts looking fuckable, you know you're in bad shape. I basically just had to lock myself in my room with nothing but photos of Lady Gaga that I looked at every time I started to think about fucking my crush. Somehow I made it through the last night of my orgasm ban.

The next morning, I woke up as excited as a kid on Christmas. As I got ready for my brunch date, I thought about turning the shower head on my neglected vag before he came to pick me up, but figured that since I had waited this long, I might as well wait to explode during sex with my London-bound lust.

I waited for him on my front porch like an eager puppy. As soon as I heard his motorcycle turn down my street, I ran out to meet him and jumped on the back of his bike, strapping my helmet on. As he revved the engine, the combination of my open legs, my tits pressed up against his back, the smell of last night's booze on his breath, and the vibrations from the bike were just too much for me. I felt the biggest orgasm of my entire life welling up inside me, and I tried to lift my cooch off the seat to stop it. It was that instant that he decided to take off, and since I wasn't securely on the bike, I fell off the back.

I had spent a month trying to prevent an orgasm, and finally found the perfect way to take my mind off sex the day I no longer needed to: a broken tail bone. That shit fucking hurt so bad I made them give me extra morphine in the hospital by starting to sob every time they tried to remove my drip. I may not have made love to my London guy, but if you've ever had the chance to do it with a hot male nurse in an adjustable hospital bed, I would lock that shit up. He even changed the sheets after.

ONE MAN'S SEXUAL HARASSER IS ANOTHER MAN'S ONE-NIGHT-STAND

If you've been strictly following the rules in this book, it's very likely that you have been accused of more than a little manhandling. But take heart my little Cuntinis, because the same behavior that may lead one man to put you on the national sex offenders registry will lead another man straight into your bed.

Early on in my slut career, I learned that grabbing an ass was a great conversation starter. Seriously, if there's ever a guy you wanna talk to in the bar but you don't know how to get his attention, just bust up on his butt and bam! Instant opener.

Of course, drunk on my ass-grabbing power, I soon grew tired of the easy pickings and the coy convo that began after feeling on butts and decided I'd challenge myself to see how much talking I could cut down if I just went straight for the peen instead. Have you ever gone to grab for something that just wasn't there? That's what happened to me one night.

My girlfriends and I were feeling particularly randy and restless after happy hour turned into happy five hours downing kamikaze shots. I wanted to get laid but wasn't sure I could even get dick in my state. I was slurring and drooling and knew witty banter was out of the question, unless I found a guy who had a thing for stroke survivors. So I decided to employ the prick grab and see what came up.

I remember looking at a male ass full of designer jeans (which was my first mistake; never trust a guy wearing girl jeans) and reached around with my hand. I was so wasted that for a second I thought I had accidentally grabbed the crotch of the blonde standing right next to him that he was hitting on.

"What the fuck, do you have a mangina*? There's nothing there!" I yelled, and in my outside voice so everyone in the bar turned around. He turned bright red and glanced at the blonde he was hoping to take home (and do what with I'm not sure because seriously, there was nothing there).

But just to make sure, I went in for another grope. "You've either done an amazing tuck job or you have just one angry inch in those girl jeans." Hearing that revelation, the blonde turned away from him and walked out. Little dude immediately started screaming to call the cops because I had assaulted him.

Now normally, I think he would just be ridiculed, then ignored, but apparently he was an investor in the bar or some shit because the next thing I knew, a squad car full of hot cops showed up and took us all outside. When someone explained what had happened, I swear I saw them stifle a laugh. They finally calmed Mr. Short Dick down and decided to haul me off to the drunk tank.

After I recovered from my vicious three-day hangover, I decided it was time to get back on the horse and headed out to another happy hour with my girls. But I was dick-shy after my bad experience, so when I saw a super-hot guy walk in the door,

I decided to downgrade my antics to ass grabbing. I headed to the bar and reached out for his Levi's-clad ass just as he started to turn around. I unintentionally got a handful of cock, and let me tell you, it was a handful. He smiled at me in a way that said this situation could also end up in cuffs—but the fur-lined kind that I had in my sex drawer.

'Course we never made it back to my house. And I still haven't gotten that sex stain off the back seat of my Prius.

TRUE OR FALSE: IS THIS SEXUAL HARASSMENT?

1. Asking to see the peen.
   a) True
   b) False

2. Commenting on what he's wearing.
   a) True
   b) False

3. Using authority to get sex.
   a) True
   b) False

4. Brushing your boobs up against him.
   a) True
   b) False

5. Sexting.
   a) True
   b) False

Answers: 1b; 2b; 3b; 4b; 5b
For the Depraved Girl, if it leads to sex, it's never sexual harassment!

IF YOU DON'T KNOW HIS GIRLFRIEND, SHE'S NOT YOUR PROBLEM

As I've said before, all is fair in sex and revenge, so when you have the chance to get with a guy you know is in a relationship, just follow this one simple rule: as long as you don't personally know his girlfriend, you have no reason not to go for him.

You may be the other woman, but if you're not in a relationship, you're not a cheat. You may not even know you're the other woman, so in that case, how can you be a cheater? Now, I won't try to pretend I don't hate on the woman who steals my man, but it's him I hold accountable; he's the cheater, she's just some unfortunate whore who's inherited my sloppy seconds.

Once I happened to be just that unfortunate whore. I had been fucking this dude who had the strangest habit of sucking his own toes to get himself turned on, but hey, whatever erects your peen.

Even though he never admitted it, I knew he had a girlfriend. How could I tell? Because there were some nights his balls smelled like Clinique Happy. Also, his Facebook status kind of gave it away. But I didn't know her, so she wasn't my problem, she was his.

On one of my fuck buddy's night's off (I assumed he was with the GF), I was having a very uncharacteristic low-key night with my girls over a couple of bottles of wine at our local dive bar when she walked in.

I could tell it was her from the obnoxious and territorial photos she would always post of herself hanging all over my fuck buddy online. A few not-so-mini-hers trailed behind her. I was fairly certain she didn't know about me, so I felt invisible enough to make fun of their Abercrombie & Fitch miniskirts, Uggs, and Juicy sweat suits to my girlfriends.

Suddenly, she and I locked eyes and she started heading toward me like a fat girl at a buffet. I looked behind me, hoping there was a Kitson kiosk behind me, but we were sitting up against a wall.

"Are you the whore who's fucking my boyfriend?" she yelled about one foot from my face as her henchwomen glared at my girls.

"Well, I'm definitely a whore, but I don't know who your boyfriend is," I lied.

My friends stood up behind me, ready to defend my dishonor, but this girl had a wild look in her eye we hadn't seen since the great syphilis outbreak of '05. Plus, we were the type of bitches who would issue a beat-down with humiliation, manipulation, and fucking shit up behind someone's back, not with a fist to a face. We were outmanned. Or outwomaned. Or out manly-womaned. (Her friends were beasts.)

I quickly surveyed the situation. It wasn't in my favor. Besides, the Depraved Girl knows that no man is worth a beat-down. "Okay, yes, I am fucking your boyfriend, but he always cries and says how much he loves you after," I said.

"Bullshit!" she exclaimed.

"Okay, yes, that was bullshit, but seriously, how in love can you be with a guy who sucks his own toes?" I asked.

She lowered her fist and laughed. "You're right, that shit is disgusting."

I offered to buy her and her crew drinks, and after our third round, we were as tight as their miniskirts. As we traded more and more stories of his sexual shortcomings, I realized that despite her horrible taste in clothes (and men), she was a kindred spirit, a fellow Depraved Girl. So I did for her what I would do for any of my other Depraved Girlfriends in a similar situation. I made it my mission to get her laid that night. (After all, the best way to get over a cheating prick is to get under another prick, right?)

We found the hottest guy in the bar and I encouraged her to follow Rule #10 and go right up to him and ask him if he wanted to fuck. She did. And then they did.

NEVER GO
TO SLEEP
HORNY

You've heard "never go to sleep angry"? Well, same thing goes for being horny. Rub it, suck it, lick it, or fuck it, but whatever you do, do not go down until you get off.

On one sweltering summer night (sans AC), I was engaged in a steamy make-out sesh with my then fuck buddy. Things got even hotter when the clothes came off and his peen came up. He was about to slip it in when we realized that we were out of condoms. My neighbor wasn't home and we were both too drunk to drive.

We tried to negotiate an oral amendment to the pussy contract, but neither of us wanted to be the giver and sixty-nine just wasn't an option because he was at least a foot taller than me. Have YOU ever tried to sixty-nine a giant? You practically need to be a yogi to get into the correct position.

Tired from the heat, the booze, and the fighting, we rolled over and went to sleep. Big mistake. Big. HUGE. The next morning I woke up in a rage. I was hot, hungover, and beyond horny.

I was angry-horny.

I yelled and screamed at him for not taking the initiative to call a cab or even go on foot to the store for a condom last night (wasn't I worth the effort?), thinking that would encourage him to rush out and grab a rubber to finish what we started. But he must have been angry-horny too, because instead of heading out to the store, he just headed out.

As soon as he left, I reached for my vibe and rubbed one out. Then I went back to sleep, a huge smile on my face. But I never did hear from Mr. Fuck Buddy again.

Going to bed without the O can be a detriment to any relationship. He may think he has a perfectly good reason not to get you off (no protection; you're on the first day of your period), but if you can't convince him to bust your nut before bed, then you might just want to take matters into your own hands. Literally.

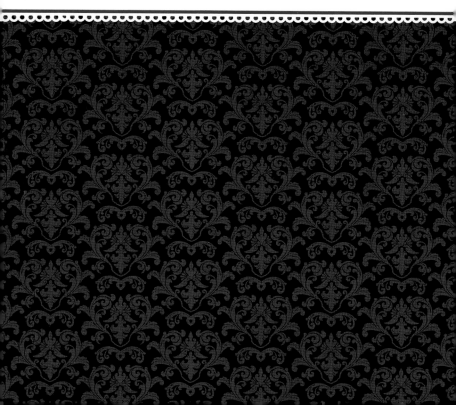

DEPRA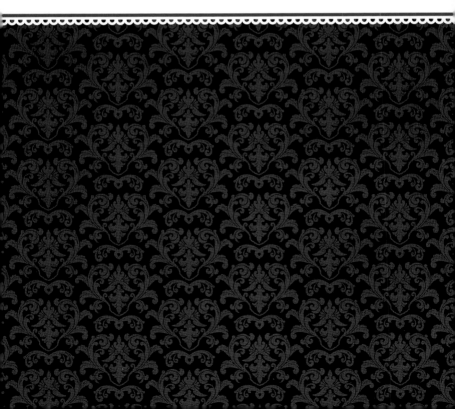VED fact

In 1993 in Sweden, a woman used the angry-horny defense to successfully dodge a murder conviction.

HOW TO HAVE CRIME SCENE SEX WITHOUT MAKING A SCENE

Ladies, we've all been there. The lust of your life is finally drunk enough to go home with you, but you're riding the crimson wave. Do you opt to go home and have a threesome with Ben and Jerry, or do you suck it up and make the best of your bloody situation? Obviously, I opt for the latter.

Let's be honest: sometimes sex on your period feels incredible. Although there are some guys who just won't get periodical with you no matter how much (or how little) you're dripping, more and more guys these days are totally into it. But you don't want to have to set up a Dexter-style kill room before he sticks it in. So here's how to work it with minimal disruption to your sexy time:

• Before you even leave the club, stick in a fresh tampon.

• As soon as you get your prey home, **give him another**

tequila shot (or two), then quickly go into the bathroom, remove the 'pon, and give your cooch a whore's bath.

- Bring a towel out of the loo with you and lay it down on the bed.

- Put the condom on and go to town. Obviously with you on top, gravity won't be helping your situation much, but chances are, he's pretty wasted at this point and won't notice when the red river starts gushing.

- As soon as he blows his load, reach for the bloody condom and grab the towel. Take them both into the bathroom, clean yourself up a little bit, then return with a warm washcloth to wash off his dick.

- At this point, he should be passed out, so feel free to use the STD flashlight you keep near your bed to see if you've missed any spots and clean them up with the washcloth.

- Insert fresh tampon and pass the fuck out!

FUCK
THE RULES

So now you've come to the end of the book, where you've been entertained, liberated, and possibly even driven to day-drink by the previous fifty-four depraved rules. You should have learned that most men are dicks, that vibrators make the best boy-friends, and that you should always fuck first and ask questions later.

If you're truly a Depraved Girl, you've just been validated by everything you've read and you're ready to graduate to varsity fucking. And like any good Depraved Girl, you make up your own rules as you go along, so fuck it and fuck on.

If you're just a tourist here, then you've probably been liberated enough to text that hot guy you've been creaming over and maybe even engage in a one-night-stand, but you'll feel guilty about it later. You're still a freshman that's probably going to get date-raped at the next kegger, so do yourself a favor and go home and read and re-read these rules over and over again until something actually sticks.

As for me? Over the last ten-plus years, I've boned through half of the dicks and douchebags in Hollywood. I've gotten fucked and fucked over, and along the way, I've collected a crew of amazing Depraved Girls who have turned out to be some of the best and most inspiring bitches I'll ever meet.

I planned on continuing to fuck my way through my puma and cougar years, knowing (and accepting) that Botox and vaginal rejuvenation surgery would have to be in the near future in order to do so—but then W came along and fucked up all my plans.

I hadn't been fucked in weeks. I kept running into all the same dirty hot dudes at my regular spots and a déjà fuck just wasn't going to do it for me anymore. I needed some fresh meat.

I decided to venture out to a friend's sister's birthday party on the West Side, hoping it would open me up to a whole new region of peen. I walked into the party, made a beeline for my girl, who was standing at the bar, and said what I usually do when I arrive at any event: "I am so fucking horny."

"You should fuck W," she said, indicating this boyishly attractive guy who was surrounded by a swarm of West Side pre-MILFs.* They were all at least five years younger than me, but light-years behind when it came to the art of getting a guy's attention.

W wasn't exactly my type (i.e., he looked like he had showered within the last twenty-four hours) and was wearing a T-shirt from a film he had worked on (gag), but I was there to broaden my vagina, so I shoved aside one of the PMILFs and told him I had heard the male lead on the film was banging little boys in his trailer during the shoot and wondered if W's butt was still sore.

The PMILFs were shocked and disgusted, but W just laughed. He dished a little dirt on the celeb's on-set behavior (mostly of the PG-13 variety) and then asked if he could buy me a drink. Now my answer, obviously, should have been "fuck yes," but W was just so nice. And we all know nice equals boring. I didn't have the energy to carry on a nice convo over my free whiskey soda, but I wasn't in the mood to be bitchy enough to ditch Opie after he paid my tab, so I just said "no, thanks" and went back to the bar.

There was no one else at the party remotely fuckable, so after my girl left to hook up with her booty call, I ended up flirting with the hipster bartender all night. Since I was still horny and tired of making love to my vibe, I went home with the bartender. The sex (like his personality) was utterly vanilla. He passed out, and while I was waiting for my cab, I noticed W had added me on Facebook, so we started chatting.

W was actually funny. This "nice boy" had a fucked-up, wicked sense of humor, and I decided then and there that he would be my backup guy. We continued our Facebook flirtation, and when my fuck buddy sprained his dick while we were doing this very complicated helicopter move, I decided to call W.

We made plans to meet at his house the next night for what I thought would be some fun NSA sex. But he actually wanted to take me out. I was a little put out because I had already pre-gamed with my vibe at home and I was ready to go, but I hadn't eaten since before my liquid lunch so I said okay, hoping he was a quick eater (of dinner AND my puss).

But W didn't fuck me that night. He didn't fuck me the next time we went out either, and before I knew it we were actually dating. Dating without fucking. Something I hadn't experienced since my good-girl days. And when we actually did have sex, it was nice. Nice and hot. I never knew that nice boys were so willing to be nasty; all you had to do was ask. Another perk of fucking a nice guy is that he was never too drunk or too fucked up on drugs, so he never got whiskey or coke dick. He wanted to have sex. All. The. Time.

I kept waiting for the other shoe to fall but it never did. One day, I woke up and realized I was in a healthy, committed relationship with a nice guy. "How the fuck did that happen?" I asked myself before promptly breaking up with him.

I went on a week-long Xantini-and-sex bender during which W called me, texted me, and Facebook-stalked me like a Depraved Girl. Since I'm not the girl I once was, when I woke up, I had a horrible hangover compounded with a bad bangover that no amount of Neosporin and anal suppositories could cure. And yet W was the one who came over to hold my hair while I puked.

We recently celebrated our third anniversary together. We were having a reverse date (you fuck first and then go out) at this little bar downtown getting wasted when I noticed a girl quietly sobbing into her cosmojito in the corner. We were getting ready to leave, so I told W to wait for me outside.

I asked the bartender for a couple of whiskeys, neat, and went over to the girl. "What did he do to you?" I asked. A fresh wave of sobs made what she said next almost unintelligible but I think it went something like this: "I think he's cheating on me with his coworker but when I confronted him he said I was crazy and he doesn't text me back for days anymore and when we have sex he seems like he just wants to get it over with and I know he's probably just not interested anymore and I should move on because I deserve better but I can't help it I love him. . . ." I handed her the whiskey and told her, "Don't cry, honey. Make him cry."

W went home alone while she and I spent the rest of the night fucking her boyfriend—and not in the good way.

Q&A WITH A DEPRAVED BITCH

A lot of very desperate people ask my advice on sex, love, and nut sack odor. Here's the best of the best.

Q: My boyfriend used to be incredibly attentive, but now he's starting to act all indifferent and he doesn't call me as much as he used to. What do I do to keep him interested?

A: Sounds like he's plotting his escape. My advice? Do it first. Tell him you want some "space" to see other people. If he still wants to be with you, he'll get jealous and become more attentive. If he doesn't, consider that a license to go on a fuck fest through half his Facebook friends list. Make sure to snap plenty of pics and tag his friends in every one.

Q: How do I get a guy to give me oral sex? What's the best way to suggest it?

A: Push his head down toward your crotch.

Q: Okay, so you know how we're always looking for the BIG cock? I've fucking found it! My lover's dick is huge! So huge it gets me sore and then I can't have sex for days. Seriously. No joke. So what the fuck should I do? All the lube and foreplay in the world isn't helping! Help! I don't want to lose this delicious man by not being able to satisfy him! I've stopped doing my Kegels.

A: Sounds like you've tapped into the myth of Moby Dick. Women like the idea of a sizable schlong because mounting a ten-incher is like a badge of honor, something to brag about to their friends. But just because you can climb Mt. Everest, doesn't mean it feels good summiting. But a Depraved Girl never backs down from a challenge, especially when it involves some delicious dick.

I suggest doing a lot of yoga to loosen up the vag muscles, and then buy yourself an inflatable butt plug. It's primarily used to loosen the ass up to get it ready for fisting, but it will work on your vagenitals in this situation as well. Start on the lowest level and insert it into your lady parts for thirty minutes a day. Every day, inflate it a little bit more until your twat can swallow the thing at its most inflated. Then swap the butt plug for your overly endowed man and fuck away.

Q: I've had threesomes before, but always with two girls and one guy, who I was in a committed relationship with. Well, now I might have the opportunity to have a threesome with two guys and one girl (my boyfriend and his best friend). My question is: how can you have a safe threesome with two guys and still have it be sexy? I am sure sucking a dude off while he has a condom on isn't the sexiest for them. I am already on the pill and I don't want to use any more contraceptives. Wouldn't condoms kind of kill the mood?

A: You know what kills the mood? STDs.

Q: My boyfriend and I have been dating for a year now and this relationship is a pretty typical heterosexual relationship. However, I'm worried because recently he's been into me playing with his asshole. Is he gay?

A: Just because your dude likes some ass play, doesn't mean that he's gay. A finger or even a fist up the butthole is also totally hetero—but once he pulls out the big black dildo, then I might start to be concerned he may not be fully playing on your team.

Q: The girl I was engaged to cheated on me for a year before I found out. How do I move on? What do I do first?

A: What you should do first is get fucked. Think of it as a palate cleanser to wash the taste of skank out of your mouth.

Q: I'm a fairly conservative woman that has recently gone through a bitter, bitter divorce and I'm just so tired of being screwed over! I've always been labeled the "nice one." I want to start fresh! I always had this fantasy of picking up some random guy at a bar for a one-night-stand, but have been afraid to do it. How would you go about doing that?

A: First, dress to get laid. If you're on a straight-up fuck mission, I'd recommend hitting the bar solo; you're more likely to be offered a free drink if you're alone. After you've gotten good and drunk off apple martinis or cosmopolitans or whatever it is you divorced ladies like to drink, ditch the loser that's been buying them for you all night and find the most fuckable man in the room. If you're new to the depraved scene, you may want to work up to coming right out and asking him if he wants to fuck, so instead just grab his ass—it's a great conversation starter.

Q: How did you go from being very sexually single to settled down? What was so great about your man to make you just want to be with him?

A: I finally found a nice guy I wanted to fuck.

Q: How do you tell your lover his balls stink?

A: I don't have time for subtleties, so I prefer the direct approach: wait until he tries to engage you in a game of BJ tug-of-war and just come out and say, "Goddamn, your balls stink like a bum on a three-day garbage bender."

Q: What separates a guy who is an average fuck from one who is amazing in bed?

A: About two to three inches.

GLOSSARY

Alkie *Noun.* Abbreviation for Alcoholic.

Bangover *Noun.* The uncomfortable to downright painful physical after-effects of too much fucking.

Breastacles *Noun.* Breasts, boobs, tittays.

Cocksessed *Adjective.* Obsessed with cock.

Cray cray *Adjective.* Crazy.

Cuddle rapist *Noun.* A person who forcibly cuddles another without consent.

Cuntini *Noun.* 1. A little cunt. 2. A Depraved Girl in training.

Déjà fuck *Verb.* The act of fucking someone you've already fucked. *Noun.* Someone you've already fucked.

Depraved Girl *Noun.* 1. An evolved female who doesn't give a shit about traditional rules. 2. A girl who wants to get laid without getting screwed. 3. The biggest cunt and most loyal bitch you'll ever meet.

Devil's threesome *Noun.* A ménage à trois with two guys and one girl.

Dress-fuck *Noun.* Being in a state of indecision about what to wear.

DSL *Adjective.* Acronym for Dick-Sucking Lips, not Digital Subscriber Line.

DTF *Adjective.* Acronym for Down to Fuck.

FJ *Noun.* Acronym for Foot Job. The act of jacking a dude off with your foot.

Fuckery *Noun.* Bullshit, shenanigans.

Fuckstravaganza *Noun.* An elaborate display of fucking.

FWB *Noun.* Acronym for Friends With Benefits.

GBF *Noun.* Acronym for Gay Best Friend.

'Gasm *Noun.* Short for Orgasm.

Gorge *Adjective.* Abbreviation for Gorgeous.

HJ *Noun.* Acronym for Hand Job. The act of jacking a dude off with your hand.

Ho-kit or **Slag-bag** *Noun.* A small bag of supplies that a ho keeps handy, stocked with one-night-stand supplies, like condoms, a toothbrush, a clean pair of panties, a pocket dildo, and Anal Eaze.

Mangina *Noun.* When a man tucks his dick between his legs, creating the illusion of a vagina.

Manties *Noun.* Men's underwear, usually of the tight-fitting, somewhat feminine variety like tightie-whities, bikini or boxer briefs.

Micro-dick *Noun.* 1. An unusually small penis measuring at about two inches erect. 2. An itsy bitsy teeny weenie.

Mr. VD *Noun.* A guy with venereal disease.

NSA *Adjective.* Acronym for No Strings Attached. The only kind of sex a Depraved Girl should engage in.

Partying with Tina *Verb.* Doing crystal meth.

PBR *Noun.* Acronym for Pabst Blue Ribbon. The hipster's ironic beer of choice.

Peen *Noun.* Penis.

Pity party *Noun.* The post-breakup party (often of one) that a woman throws for herself after she's been dumped. Usually involves large quantities of frozen desserts, Xanax, and red wine.

Prairie-dogging *Verb.* When you have to take a shit so bad but there's no toilet in sight, your poo starts popping its head in and out of your anus.

Pre-MILF or **PMILF** *Noun.* 1. A woman who you would think was hot for someone who just popped a couple of kids out of her cooch, but since her womb has yet to be occupied is only just okay. 2. MILF is an acronym for Mother I'd Like to Fuck.

Rex *Noun.* Abbreviation for Anorexic.

RJ *Noun.* Acronym for Rim Job. 1. The act of licking a guy's bunghole. 2. What usually happens after a guy gives a girl Chanel.

Roofie colada *Noun.* When you drop a roofie into a mixed drink, no matter what the drink, it becomes a roofie colada.

Slag-bag *Noun.* (See: Ho-kit.)

Slutspertise *Noun.* Expert skill or knowledge in a particular slut field.

Slutventures *Noun.* Slutty adventures.

Stalkapalooza *Noun.* A marathon stalking-fest that spans several days and locations.

Stuck good *Verb.* When you're fucked really good and really hard.

The pit *Noun.* That horrible anxious, empty feeling in your stomach that can only be filled with Xanax, alcohol, or a rebound fuck.

Thrill fucker *Verb.* Having sex in unusual/thrilling places, situations, and combinations, and getting off on the thrill of it.

Vag *Noun.* Abbreviation for Vagina.

Vagenitals *Noun.* Female genitalia.

Vajazzled *Verb.* The act of bedazzling your beaver with crystals.

Vibe *Noun.* 1. Abbreviation for Vibrator. 2. Woman's best friend.

Vikes *Noun.* Abbreviation for the painkiller Vicodin.

Whore's bath *Noun.* When one washes only one's essential body parts (crotch and armpits) before a night of whoring.

Xantini *Noun.* 1. Xanax washed down with a martini. 2. The most amazing thing ever invented.

ACKNOWLEDGMENTS

Thanks to all my Depraved Girls and Gays who either intentionally or unintentionally contributed to this book. (You're welcome for not using your real names.) Thanks to Niki Savage, who recognized the value in this project when I didn't, and funded countless hours of "research"; my amazing editor, Jordana Tusman, my book designer, Corinda Cook, and publicists Craig Herman and Seta Zink, and everyone at Running Press; the best reps a Depraved Girl could have: Brandi Bowles at Foundry Media, Brad Mendelsohn, Eric Feig, Lindsay Howard, and Melissa Orton; my great friend and publicist, Jason Mitchell; Bob Conte and everyone at HBO; an honorary Depraved Girl, Creighton Rosental, who gave me help and inspiration at the end when I needed it the most; and my family, who greatly contributed to my delinquency, in more ways than one. And most of all, I want to thank Brad Skiles, without whom I would never have finished this book. Thanks for having never made me use any of these rules on you—yet.

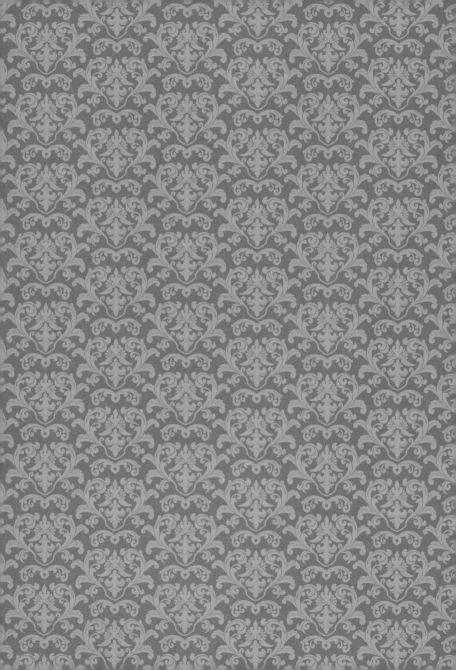